ACRYLIC

FOR SCULPTURE AND DESIGN

Clarence Bunch, column.

CLARENCE BUNCH

ACRYLIC
FOR SCULPTURE AND DESIGN

VNR VAN NOSTRAND REINHOLD COMPANY
NEW YORK CINCINNATI TORONTO LONDON MELBOURNE

Van Nostrand Reinhold Company Regional Offices:
New York Cincinnati Chicago Millbrae Dallas
Van Nostrand Reinhold Company International Offices:
London Toronto Melbourne

Copyright © 1972 by Litton Educational Publishing, Inc.
Library of Congress Catalog Card Number 75-149251

Published by Van Nostrand Reinhold Company
450 West 33rd Street, New York, N.Y. 10001
Published simultaneously in Canada by
Van Nostrand Reinhold Limited
16 15 14 13 12 11 10 9 8 7 6 5 4 3 2 1

ACKNOWLEDGMENTS

Acrylic for Sculpture and Design owes a great deal to a good many people. I would like to thank Dr. Edwin Ziegfeld for his invaluable advice and guidance, John Lidstone for causing me to see the possibility of my work being the basis of a book and for setting up the initial interview with the publisher, and Ted Johnson for his phenomenal patience and dedicated work beyond his usual editing duties. There are too many other people to thank individually for their varied suggestions and services. I am especially grateful to the artists and gallery and museum directors who supplied photographs and bibliographic material. Also I would like to express my appreciation and thanks to friends who tolerated me with much understanding and some amusement during the period this book came into being.

PHOTOGRAPH CREDITS

A number of the photographs used in this book were made available by the Museum of American Crafts of the American Crafts Council, which held an exhibition, "Plastic as Plastic," from November 23, 1968, to January 12, 1969. The exhibition was something of a milestone for acrylic sculpture and crafts, and it was a great convenience to me to have this source for photographs of the work of many of the artists I wanted to discuss.

Where a single credit is given for a page that has more than one illustration, all the illustrations on the page are from the same source.

CONTENTS

PREFACE

In preparing this book, and making choices of items to illustrate and discuss, I have continually been reminded that acrylic, although in existence since 1934, is just now coming into common use by artists and designers and that most other people seem hardly to know that it exists. It is understandable that the general public is confused by the many varieties of plastics available. Perhaps no one should be expected to have a detailed knowledge of acrylic, and in fact many know so little about it that they substitute the trade name "Plexiglas" or "Lucite" or "Perspex" for the word "acrylic." But the material deserves to be better known.

It is my intention to show some of the many ways acrylic is being used and to suggest, indirectly, further ways that it might be used by artists, designers, and laymen. I have tried to explain how the material is worked so that even a complete beginner can use it successfully. There is no mystery in working acrylic—though there is a great deal of mystery in the objects created, despite the cool objectivity of the resin.

The first chapter of this book is a general introduction to acrylic. The second chapter is concerned with acrylic sculpture. The third chapter is on acrylic furniture and jewelry. The final chapter is a detailed description of tools and processes used to work the material. There is a short Afterword about my own experience with acrylic and my feelings for it.

The section on sculpture is quite long, because I believe it is here that the best use of the material occurs, and because commercial designers have followed the lead of sculptors. There is no architecture section, since acrylic is not being used architecturally to any extent, possibly because the material scratches easily and because it is too expensive in large quantities. Perhaps in the future when chemists at DuPont or Rohm and Haas have perfected an acrylic that approaches the hardness of glass, and the material is no longer priced out of reason, it will come into more regular use.

I must admit that I don't like acrylic furniture. If I think of it as sculpture I often find it spectacular and beautiful. But the fingerprints and smudges left by those who use it as furniture would annoy me; if I had an acrylic chair in my studio I would constantly be cleaning it with antistatic spray. I would worry about scratches too. The beauty of acrylic is its high sheen and gloss, and once it has lost that sheen it looks drab and cheap. Perhaps some day acrylic furniture will be used for a few

R. Buckminster Fuller's geodesic dome for Expo has a skin of thermo-formed acrylic panels—one of the few ambitious uses of the material architecturally.

months or years, like a disposable flashlight, and then melted down and recycled, but at the moment it is much too expensive for recycling. And even if one were to solve the other problems, an acrylic chair would never seem stable to me. The material is very strong, but it does have a springiness that makes me uneasy.

And yet—it is beautiful. Acrylic furniture can enlarge areas and transform rooms. (Often it is presented to the public by merchandisers in wildly futuristic settings, in which few of us live; actually it is often more interesting and effective when combined with traditional materials and furniture.) It can delight the user when it is good and bore him when it is bad. It is at the very least a use of the material that is worth exploring further.

All in all this is a general book rather than a close study, a selective survey rather than a comprehensive catalog. Many excellent sculptors and designers are not included here, simply because there was not room for them or because there were no good photographs of their work available. The book is intended to explain existing interest in acrylic, to generate more interest in it, and above all to encourage first-hand experience with it.

1. THE MATERIAL

PLASTIC

Plastic is the twentieth century's only new material. It speaks to us of rocket ships and moon landings, as well as of disposable dishes. It exemplifies modern man's invention of planned obsolescence while remaining as ambiguous and mysterious as life itself. It is a material that in a remarkably short time has revolutionized our approach to life. And since it is so much a part of daily existence, it attracts the attention of artists, designers, and craftsmen.

The dictionary defines plastic as a material "capable of being molded or of receiving form." Such a definition, however, is much too simple to cover the variety of plastic materials available today. The definition is based merely on a transient property plastic has during the process of manufacture; it does not take into consideration specific properties of the numerous synthetic materials. It is a commercial rather than a scientific term.

As a generic word, "plastic" designates a general category of materials only, as do the words "wood" and "metal." As it is possible to recognize different types of woods and metals, so it is possible to recognize different materials labeled as plastics.

Industry started using "plastic" as a name rather casually in the 1920's, when the word began to appear in technological indexes to cover the family of new materials made possible by chemistry. At that time, it was felt that plasticity was the only common element (an obviously important feature of the various synthetic materials), and the name stuck.

There are two main types of plastics: thermoplastics and thermosetting plastics. A piece of thermoplastic will retain the structural character of a solid even while undergoing physical change caused by heat and pressure, and it may be reshaped any number of times. Acrylic is a thermoplastic. A thermosetting plastic, on the other hand, may be shaped only once.

Thermoplastics retain their structural character because they are in an amorphous state of matter rather than in a crystalline state. In the crystalline state, matter is arranged in an orderly fashion, while in the amorphous state, the arrangement is random. In the case of plastics, this condition is due to the fact that they are polymers: giant molecules made up of numerous small, relatively simple repeating units of atoms combined into molecular chains of great length that are not capable of being arranged in a compact ordered manner.

At the initial stage in its history (and in some plastics at later times) a plastic is capable of flow, and with the application of adequate heat and pressure it can be caused to take a desired shape which will be retained when the temperature and pressure are withdrawn.

When crystalline materials are heated, no change in state occurs until the melting point is reached, at which time, of course, complete liquefaction takes place. In the case of thermoplastics, an increase in temperature permits increased mobility of the molecular chains with an increasing ability to flow under pressure, without any conspicuous change in state.

By contrast with other materials that can be made to flow and can be shaped under heat and pressure, such as metal and glass, plastic has one outstanding characteristic: it is derived from organic products or compounds in which the element carbon is the principal structural unit. Plastics are synthetic substances produced from organic materials based on carbon chemistry. They are made or synthesized by chemical means from simple organic raw materials converted into radically different forms.

ACRYLIC PLASTIC

Acrylic plastic is produced through a series of intricate chemical processes involving organic compounds based on coal and oil, such as hydrocyanic acid, methanol, and acetone. The interaction of these, with water and air, forms gases, which, in turn, are converted under pressure to a clear colorless liquid with a viscosity, specific gravity, and general appearance similar to water. The clear, water-thin liquid, methyl methacrylate, is a monomer made up of tiny molecules which, under proper chemical control, unite to form a "polymer." In the case of acrylic the polymer solidifies into a hard, rigid, transparent, solid. The action of polymerization is generally effected by heat, pressure, and catalysts such as acid or ether peroxides. Careful and constant chemical control is required to polymerize a monomer. The particular polymer that concerns us, acrylic, is composed of hydrogen, oxygen, and carbon.

Solid acrylic forms are made by solidification of acrylic resin in suitably shaped glass molds, or by pouring the thick liquid between parallel sheets of plate glass to produce the more common flat sheets. Sheets and slabs of all sizes, as well as rods, are made in this manner. To make colored forms and sheets, dyes or pigments are added to the casting resin.

This cast thermoplastic, acrylic, can be produced in several formulations to provide specific properties for different applications by altering the formula of the ingredients that constitute it, and by modifying the process used in its production. Acrylic plastic is available under the trade names Acrylite, Crystalite, Lucite, and Plexiglas in the United States, Altuglas in France, and Perspex in Great Britain.

Acrylic is also available in the form of emulsions and syrups which are used for casting and in painting.

SPECIAL CHARACTERISTICS OF ACRYLIC

Solid acrylic has characteristics that make it unusually well adapted to art and craft work. It is a rigid, lightweight material (one of the lightest of the plastics) only one-third to one-half as heavy as aluminum. Acrylic possesses high tensile strength, making it comparable to wood in bending ability, although it is only about one-third as stiff as structural lumber.

It is as hard as other thermoplastics. It is not as hard as glass, but it has an impact strength ten to seventeen times greater. Despite its fragile glasslike appearance, acrylic is shatter-resistant and difficult to break except by hard direct blows. Heat transfer through the material is approximately 20 percent less than through the equivalent thickness of glass. It is odorless in its solid state and warm to the touch. Acrylic is not affected by alkalis, oils, greases, nonoxidizing acids, dilute alcohol, or most household chemicals.

The material has a high resistance to weathering and other aging properties, showing no dimensional changes when subjected to wide variations in humidity and temperature conditions, although the clear plastic may show slight yellowing after prolonged exposure to sunlight. It is difficult to ignite even in an open flame and when ignited has a slow burning rate.

There are two types of sheets available: shrunk and unshrunk acrylic. Shrunk acrylic sheets are manufactured to exacting standards of optical clarity, surface finish, and thickness tolerances, and they remain stable throughout thermoforming operations. Unshrunk sheets shrink about 2 percent when heated to forming temperature. Unshrunk acrylic is less expensive than shrunk acrylic, and for this reason it is more suitable for use where heat is not a factor, or in thermoforming operations where shrinkage is of little concern.

Solid acrylic is a tough and durable material with excellent machining properties. It can be sawed, drilled, polished, and, in general, worked like wood or soft metals. In addition, the material can be formed by heat into almost any shape. It has unusual adhesive properties so that parts may be cemented in strong bonds without discernible joints. It takes paint and dyes and is highly impermeable to moisture.

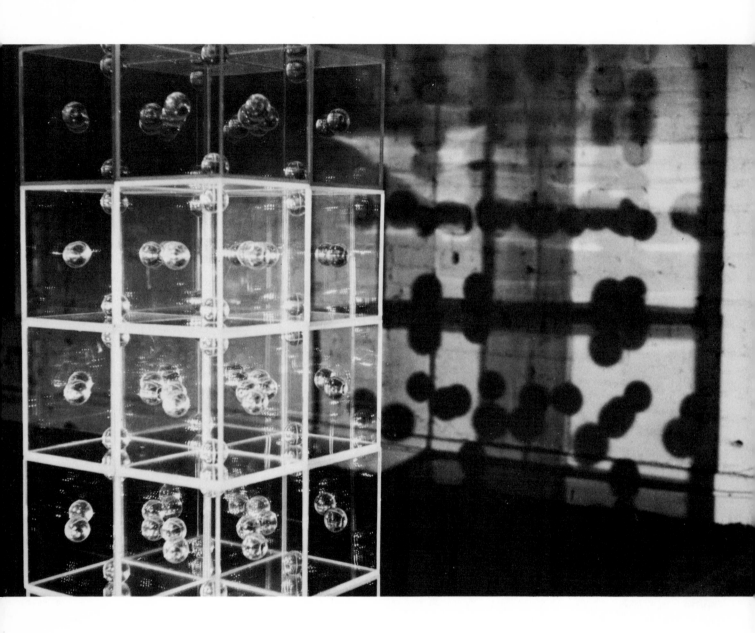

Acrylic accepts light uniquely. In this modular piece the bottom section glows from a direct bright light. The top part seems to disappear because it is indirectly lighted. Edges and spheres are edge-lighted and cast shadows, even though they are as transparent as the sheets themselves.

Transparency & light

In addition to being well suited for the construction of sculpture and design and craft objects because of its toughness and its machining and thermoforming capabilities, acrylic has many aesthetic attributes that make it an exciting material. In the first place, it is a product of our own age—it has no tradition of art use behind it, and so it frees the artist, craftsman, and designer of any culturally inbred ideas of "what is possible." But its special virtue is its transparency.

Light transmission through acrylic is substantially better than with even the finest optical glass. The thicker a piece of glass, the less light is transmitted; thus, it is difficult to see any object through glass which is more than six inches thick. On the other hand, articles seen through slabs of acrylic three feet thick are as clear as if nothing were intervening. This ideal light diffusion, or almost perfect transparency, frees acrylic from image distortion and makes it extraordinarily brilliant. The crystal clarity of the material allows the transmission of both visible and ultraviolet light.

In its clear form acrylic can be either transparent or highly reflective to light. It can be almost invisible, or it can reflect light and images much as a mirror does. The material's transparency or reflectivity depends on the source and amount of light.

Light entering at one edge of a piece of acrylic will be efficiently transmitted to the other edges, even around corners. When light enters acrylic, it is reflected from the inside surface of the material, and these reflections come out at the polar end with minor ambient loss—the visual characteristics of a diamond. The edges, and roughened areas, where a surface is broken, will glow, while the rest of the sheet remains almost invisible. This characteristic is sometimes called edge-lighting.

Light is an integral part of the material itself, not an element imposed on it. Artists are using both natural and artificial light as aesthetic and artistic properties, structural elements or units, almost as one would use a piece of the material to form or fabricate a piece of sculpture or furniture. Light in acrylic is a basic element of art; a more tangible artistic property than it has ever been before. This will be quite apparent to the reader as he examines the works pictured in this book.

Limitations of acrylic

With all these advantages, acrylic has certain limitations. Although it is resistant to corrosion from most household chemicals, the surface of the material can be attacked, crazed, or dissolved by many liquids and their vapors: aromatic hydrocarbons, esters, chlorinated hydrocarbons, certain lower alcohols; and aromatic solvents, paint solvents, and dopes and thinners such as turpentine, benzene, toluene, lacquer thinner, acetone, and ketones. The resistance to many of these chemicals will depend on their concentration and the temperature and stress imposed on the acrylic during exposure.

Acrylic is one of the hardest of the thermoplastics, but it is susceptible to scratching. Scratches are more apparent on clear, transparent acrylic than on the opaque variety. Scratches can be buffed and polished until no longer apparent, although this is tedious.

Further, the material has a tendency to attract dust because of static electricity. There are antistatic cleaners on the market that help the material to reject particles of dust and dirt for a time after application. These antistatic solutions will also help clean the surface. Acrylic is usually cleaned with a mild soap or detergent with water and wiped dry with a soft cloth or chamois.

It is wise for the artist or designer to keep the limitations of acrylic in mind—both its physical and its aesthetic limitations—as he would with any medium. This is sometimes difficult with acrylic, because the material tempts one. Thus artist Billy Omabeglio constructed a magnificent acrylic staircase. Acrylic is perfectly transparent and can be bonded almost invisibly; the same result could not have been achieved with glass. So it is a proper and successful use of the material. But if the object is thought of not as sculpture but as a staircase—if it is being viewed by an engineer rather than a gallery-goer—it is almost shockingly improper, like the Dadaist fur teacup and saucer.

Billy Omabeglio's staircase is set in a mirrored stairwell over a mirrored floor. It is beautiful to look at and sensational to use; a friend of the artist's is shown in cautious descent. However, the material scratches easily. The treads are protected with clear vinyl.

2.
ACRYLIC IN TWENTIETH-CENTURY SCULPTURE

There are no images or other references to the outside world in much acrylic sculpture. For the most part artists working with the material deal strictly with visual phenomena, and the work is literal. Their intent more often than not seems to be to create beautiful and fascinating objects that are mysterious, yet contain an objective reality. Generally such individual pieces are as different for each viewer as it is possible for the creator to make them. They are objects which can and should be viewed on a wide variety of levels.

As has already been pointed out, light is an expressive quality with which the sculptor deals when working with acrylic. Much acrylic work contains interior artificial lights that function as an integral part of the sculpture. However, external lighting is also common and is sometimes more interesting. Projected colored light is used occasionally and offers endless possibilities for change and viewer participation. The fact that a transparent piece can be made to glow and appear subtle or brilliant due to light intensity is exciting and offers opportunity for much variety in sculptural work.

Varying the light system, lighting the work indirectly or directly with floods or spots, or changing the color of the light bulb or filter can alter the appearance of the piece. Indeed, the entire environment can be altered. The same piece illuminated with a pink light has a much different presence than when illuminated with a blue light. Either the sculptor or the viewer can regulate the "meaning" of acrylic work through the use of lights that are colored or clear, intense or dim. One more possibility for change has been added, one more step the viewer can take in creating his own "sculpture."

Natural light changes that occur as a day passes are more personal and intensely felt than artificial light changes. The work becomes as private and immediate as a plant in a room.

Opaque color is not of central importance in most acrylic work. It is secondary to the kinetic aspects, to the transparency and reflective qualities of acrylic and to the way it accepts light. Somehow, solid color seems an artificial element, a little alien to the material. Too great a use of solid color tends to distort acrylic's purity. Solid color appears more often as an accessory or accent.

Many artists' acrylic work seems to have more in common with painting than with sculpture. Perhaps this is because they painted before they began to work with acrylic. However, it seems more likely that there are elements in the material itself that call forth painterly discoveries, ideas, and solutions to three-dimensional problems. The fact that most contemporary artists discussed here have also turned to three-dimensional work in acrylic from painting and have used no other materials in their sculptural work would reinforce this contention.

The Earliest Acrylic Sculptors: Gabo, Pevsner, and the Constructivists

In their *Realistic Manifesto* of 1920, Naum Gabo and Antoine Pevsner declared: "We deny volume as an expression of space. We reject physical mass as an element of plastic art." This statement may seem mysterious at first glance, but it is far from meaningless. The *Manifesto* was a short, pointed document written in opposition to Vladimir Tatlin and other Russian artists who held the view that art was dead and the artist must serve the Revolution. The *Manifesto* denied this, and affirmed that what was needed was a new art form. Gabo and Pevsner expressed their conviction that there is a general intellectual principle which applies to the use of a given material or technical process. They hoped to illuminate current ideas in art and release them to contemporary philosophic and scientific thought through the use of modern industrial materials and processes. Volume and mass were to be rejected in favor of space and movement, and time and space to be considered fundamental elements of art as well as life. A piece of sculpture was to be penetrated on all sides by space and light. It was no longer to be an opaque silhouette. Thus Gabo and Pevsner systematized what philosopher-critic Michel Seuphor has called the "active void."

It was the Constructivists' contention that sculpture is intentionally built in three-dimensional space of concrete material, and is created to make visible the emotions of the artist. Gabo stated: "These are the main attributes which we find in every sculptural work since the art of sculpture began, and which distinguish a sculptural work from any other object. Any other attributes which appear are of secondary and temporary nature and do not belong to the basic substance of sculpture."

From the beginning, Gabo chose to work with materials of the scientific age—materials rarely or never used by sculptors in his day. His first works were done in cardboard and metal, but he found that the new transparent plastics were particularly well suited to his ideas. He produced the first example of an entirely new kind of art work: construction. He used plastics (originally celluloid and later acrylic) in sculpture that, according to the art historian Alan Browness, "owed more to the Eiffel Tower and the Crystal Palace than to Michelangelo or Rodin." Gabo, who had a mathematical background and engineering training, employed an architectural conception of space in his constructions, as did his fellow Constructivists.

Left:

Antoine Pevsner, "Torso" (1924-6), 29½" high. The transparent plastic and the opaque copper echo each other.

Opposite:

Naum Gabo, "Column" (1923), 41½" high. The piece incorporates wood and metal as well as plastic.

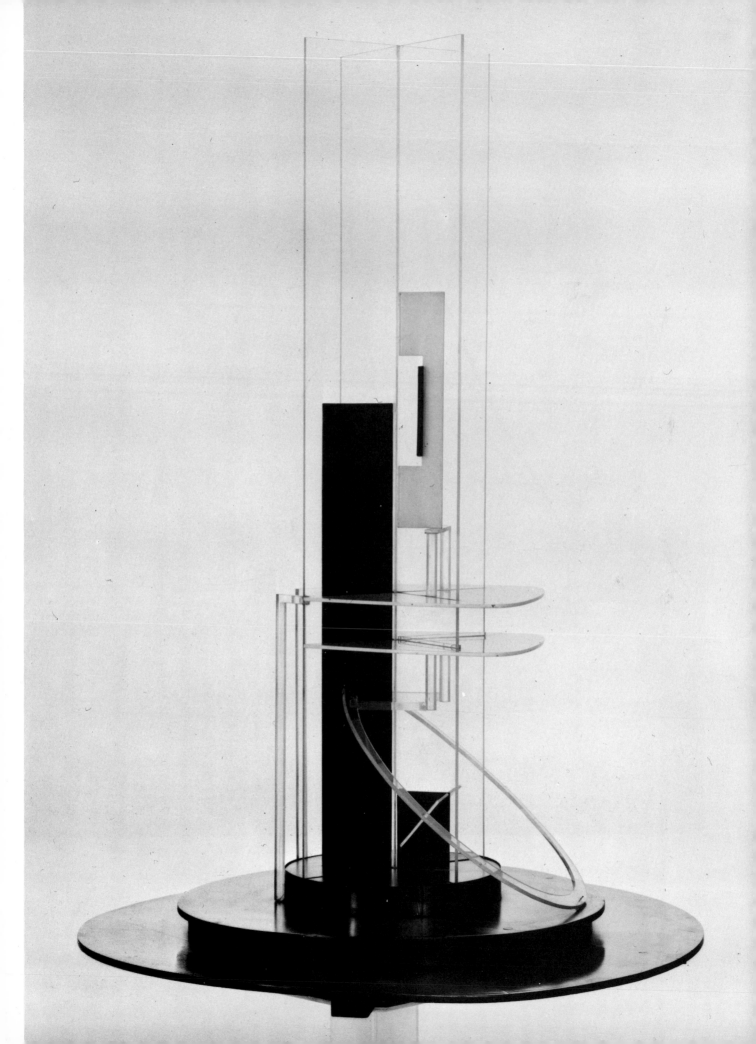

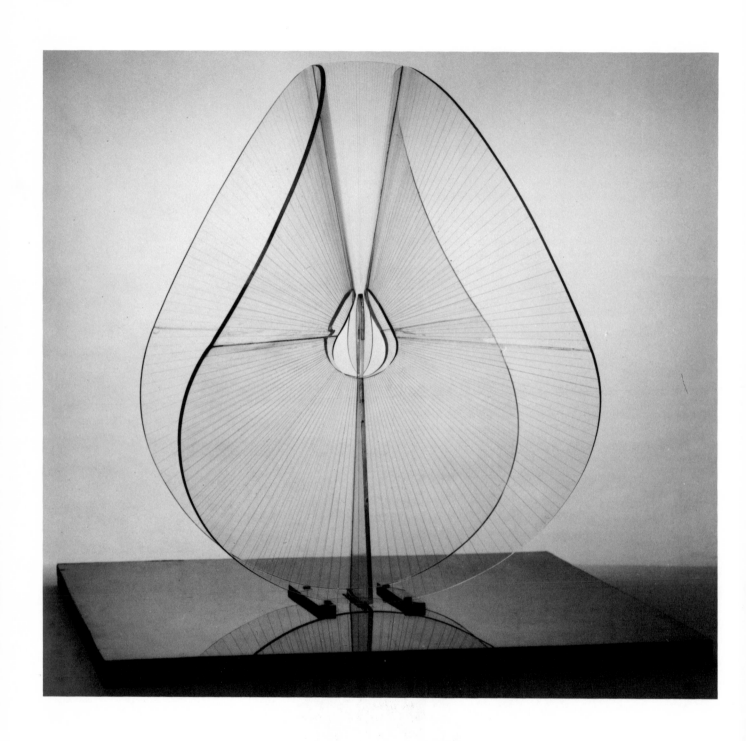

Naum Gabo, "Translucent Variation on Spheric Theme" (1951 version of 1937 original), 22⅜" high. The piece is mainly a single oval sheet of clear acrylic. Lines were incised radiating from the center open core to the outside edge, and then the sheet was thermoformed. It is supported over a reflective base by a vertical shaft of acrylic.

He searched for the possibilities of the new materials in relation to his concern with light and its exploration. He and the Constructivist group spoke for new ways in art to give expression to the new and expanded conception of the universe.

Gabo, Pevsner, and other Constructivists abandoned traditional approaches to sculpture. They planned in advance, cut and worked the pieces, and assembled the assorted parts in order to form the completed work. As their acknowledged leader, Gabo, said: "We call ourselves Constructivists because we no longer paint our pictures or carve our sculptures, and because both are 'constructed' in space and with the help of space. Thus we break down the old distinction between painting and sculpture. By way of the Constructivist principle the visual arts enter the domain of 'architecture'; by architecture I mean not only the building of houses, but the whole edifice of our everyday existence."

A. L. Chanin, writing in *Art News* about Gabo's work, made a useful observation about Constructivist aesthetics: "Constructivist sculpture presents non-static images constructed in space; space is an actual, plastic, immediate element of the sculpture, and thus air also becomes a part of the substance of the work, strikingly enhanced by a stress on transparent materials. Constructivist images seek to express our age of science..."

And Herbert Read, also commenting on Gabo, tried to place the movement in the larger cultural frame: "His constructions are not *objets d'art* for the connoisseur—they do not belong in any sense to the bourgeois tradition of art. They are images of a tradition that has still to be established—prototypes of an art that is emerging to give expression to the unformulated ideals and blind aspirations of a new age. New materials, new processes, a new technology of unknown potentiality, are waiting to be fused by the imagination of a new breed of artists into the monuments of a new civilization."

Gabo's constructions, like many of those of other Constructivists, are clean, uncluttered, and classical in feeling. They allow no place for association or autobiography. They are rational structures: abstract in content, concerned with balance, proportion, rhythm, and movement. They introduce a new reality into nonobjective sculpture. The work of the Constructivists identified a new spirit in art and a new artist, one who fused industrial materials and modern concepts of time, form, and space. This new artist took his cue from the industrial world, and the feeling of light and movement gave his work a positive thrust into the future.

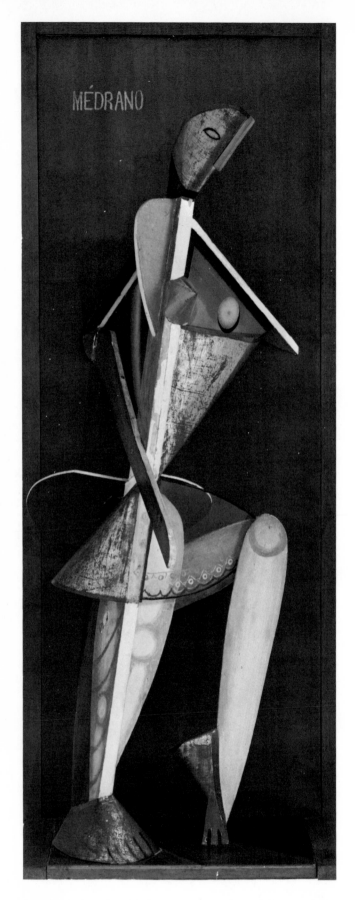

MÉDRANO

Alexander Archipenko, "Médrano" (1915), 49½" high. This very early work was made of painted metal, wood, oilcloth, and glass—acrylic was still many years in the future.

Alexander Archipenko

Even before World War I, Alexander Archipenko built figures composed of abstract geometric forms reminiscent of mechanical parts, and long before Assemblages were thought of, he combined painting with sculpture. His experiments with space, which use concave and convex shapes that define or hide and confuse space with form, make his artistic and aesthetic bent ideally suited for the twentieth century's revolutionary material. Archipenko recalled, "As early as 1912, I felt the need for experimentation with *transparency*, but was limited to the only transparent material available at that time—glass." He began using acrylic in 1947 as a sculptural medium, and his acrylic work illustrates his ideas of creation as spirit united with matter within the continually evolving human body, and what he refers to as "planetary forces." The scientific spirit of the twentieth century had, and has, its poetic side too.

The critic Katherine Kuh tells us that "his greatest contribution was metaphysical. He made what is seem what is not. It was the duality of vision that interested him, less the image itself than our reaction to the image. Turning total voids into solid form, he also discovered that surrounding space could become as potent as dense mass." Archipenko himself said: "Plastic illuminated from within produces an ethereal quality. Transparent Plexiglas produces the effect of an esoteric substance, unlike wood or marble with their materiality of surface. Transparent plastic evokes the idea of abstraction rather than the harsh positiveness of nontransparent materials."

Speaking of an exhibition of Archipenko's lighted acrylic work, the art historian Karl Silex said: "Then one comes into the dark room illuminated by the glow of the Plexiglas structures. The currents of energy here are currents of light. The light penetrates the room in all directions, but still it does not illuminate. The Plexiglas suggests the dematerialization of matter."

Archipenko's use of an electric light, located in the sculptural pedestal, to edge-light and illuminate his acrylic sculpture has its roots in his concern for the play of natural light in his earlier work. The *Medrano* of 1915 was his first experiment with transparency (he used a piece of glass in the construction) and is an excellent example of his concern with the shifting, evasive, and continually changing quality of light that was to be of primary interest to him in the 1940's and 1950's.

Archipenko was one of the few artists working with acrylic who carved the material. Most have chosen to work in a Constructivist manner rather than use a traditional carving approach. Also, he was one of the few to work in acrylic figuratively. Most artists seem to feel that nonobjective forms best express the quality of the material. As Archipenko explained his technique: "I apply entirely different principles

Archipenko in his studio, working a lump of acrylic with a machine he invented to carve the material.

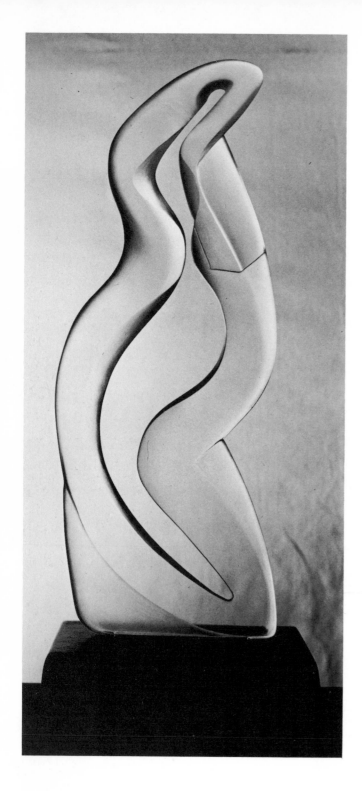

Alexander Archipenko, "She Is the Space." The original acrylic piece (1947) is shown here lighted by natural light and also lighted internally. The drawing (about 1948) was made as a study from the sculpture. The bronze (1960; cast from the acrylic) has an entirely different feeling; texture and reflection take the place of transparency.

 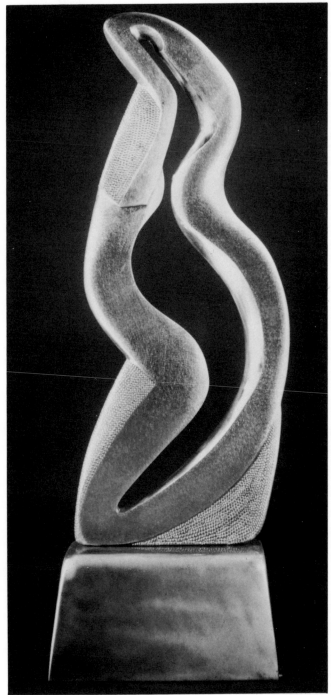

than heretofore practiced. For my purpose I use a thick sheet of Plexiglas and carved forms on both sides and adjust their interdependencies in order to obtain unity of form from both views. The three-dimensional character of the flat material I obtain either by actually twisting the planes of the material or by designing and carving the figure in foreshortening or perspective. I use Plexiglas and Lucite and new technical methods in order to model four elements: light, transparency, space and the concave. This brings a new aesthetic expression."

Archipenko was committed to constant change in life as well as in his work, and his restless nature is reflected in his acrylic sculpture. Although calm at first glance, the sculptures are continually changing, continually shifting as the viewer moves about looking at them. Indeed, they demand that the viewer be active; a shift of several inches to the right or left will open up a completely new artistic world. Our consciousness is expanded and our life is enriched, for we have been drawn into the work to experience, as directly as possible, the artist's creative action. Archipenko has accomplished this by making a sculpture that contains his spirit—his restlessness as well as his intellect—and by forcing us to move physically.

As Karl Silex explained it, "Archipenko demands creative participation on the part of the beholder. [He] fashions his material only to the point where it sends forth currents of energy which for him are the important thing. Hence the beholder is obliged to supplement what he sees..."

Alexander Archipenko, "People," an architectural screen. The pencil sketch was a study for the piece.

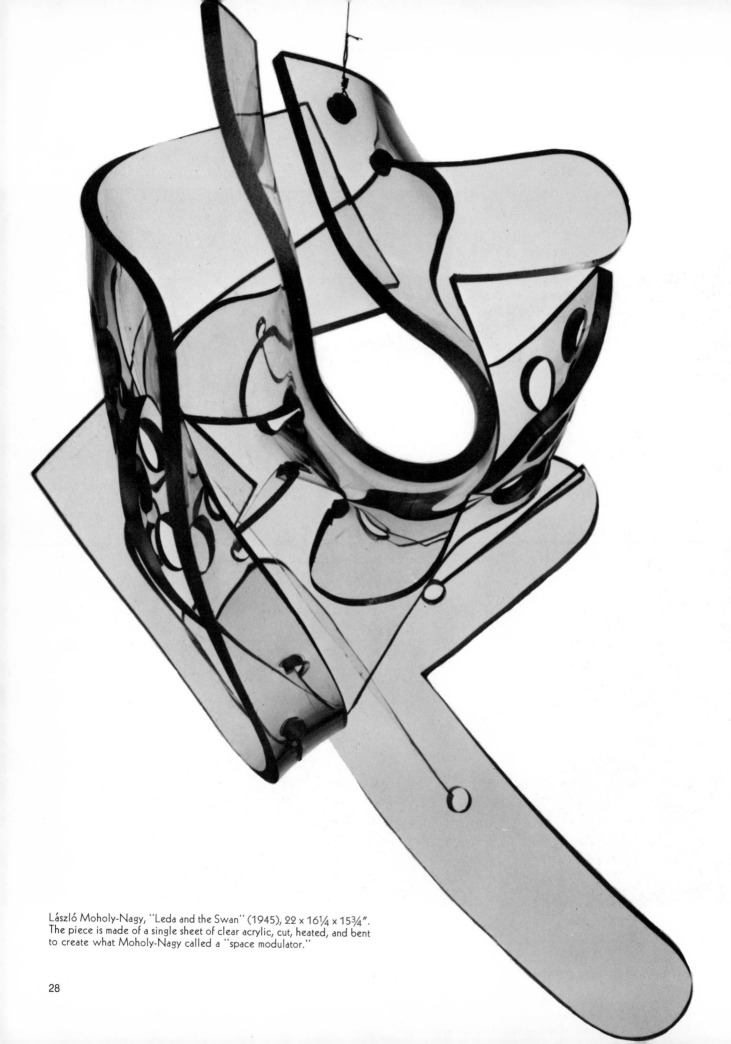

László Moholy-Nagy, ''Leda and the Swan'' (1945), 22 x 16¼ x 15¾".
The piece is made of a single sheet of clear acrylic, cut, heated, and bent
to create what Moholy-Nagy called a ''space modulator.''

László Moholy-Nagy

Another early experimenter with plastic was László Moholy-Nagy, one of the original Bauhaus group that experimented with new materials and abstract forms in an effort to relate the arts more closely to the sciences. He was interested in tensions and forces as motives in his work, and he made sculpture, as he said, "to dissolve solid volume and to define space."

Moholy-Nagy replaced volume and mass with light and movement. In the 1930's his work was almost exclusively devoted to "space modulators," done with acrylic sheet which he thermoformed into complex shapes, usually each made from a single piece.

The art historian Addison F. Page, in discussing Moholy-Nagy's work, expressed in a very few words one of the mysteries of acrylic sculpture—its simultaneous human appeal and independence from nature. He said Moholy-Nagy "has caught something of the random quality of ordinary human movement in the free plasticity of his material, and its transparency allows us to be aware of forms, textures, and space simultaneously. His space modulator represents a very fluid idea of what sculpture can accomplish, far removed from any traditional concepts of solid monumentality and the reproduction of any form that would appear in nature."

His influence spread to the United States in 1938, when he brought the Bauhaus concept from Germany to Chicago. He taught an empirical method of investigation for the production of art, and his students learned functional and constructional possibilities using a wide range of materials. He was preoccupied with the contrast of materials, the relationship of geometric forms, mathematical precision, and the "newness" of the materials used. He believed that when one discovered constructional aspects of a material, he had also discovered its aesthetic possibilities.

Just before his death, Moholy-Nagy expressed his commitment to the new vision when he stated: "It is the artist's duty today to penetrate yet unseen ranges of biological functions,

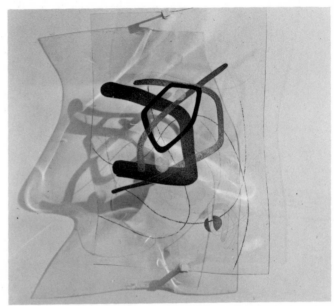

László Moholy-Nagy, relief wall piece. It is a sheet of acrylic shaped by heat and painted. In great part it depends on shadow for its effectiveness.

to search the new dimensions of the industrial society and to translate the new findings into emotional orientation."

Moholy's influence remains strong today, when pure idea is more important than craft or execution, which is often carried out by technicians working from the artist's designs, if brought into being at all. *Newsweek* quotes Sybil Moholy-Nagy, his widow, about *Em 1*, created in 1922: "To show that his pure forms could be easily understood, he once called up the foreman of a factory and dictated to him the dimensions and simple motifs of a work and asked the foreman to create it. It came out just as he wanted. It was the first example of telephone art."

László Moholy-Nagy, "Prehistoric Construction" (1942), 10 x 24⅞". It is a painting, but on an incised piece of ¼-inch acrylic rather than canvas.

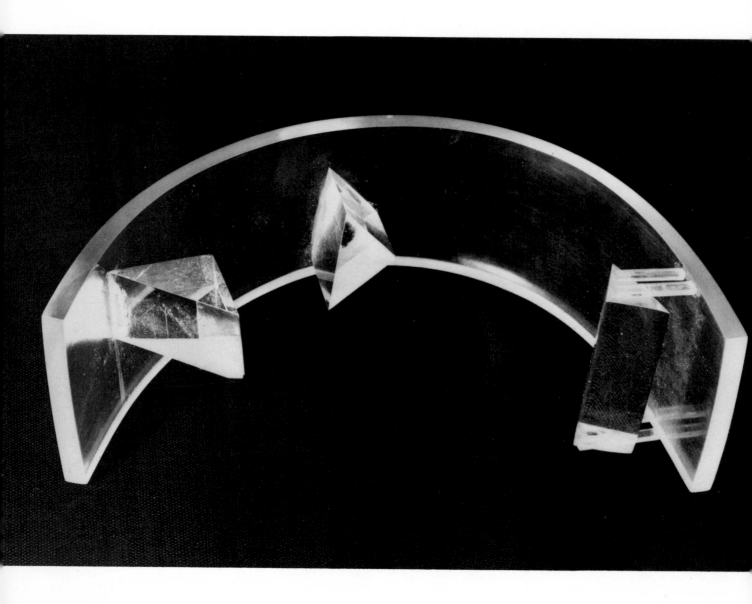

Above:

Georges Vantongerloo, "Transformer la lumière en couleur" (1959; "To transform light into color"), 8¼" long. This piece has three prisms set at different angles to produce spectral colors.

Opposite:

Georges Vantongerloo, "Couleur par refraction" (1952; "Color by refraction"), 8¼" high. The thermoformed rod within the cylinder was spotted with color, which is distorted and magnified in complex ways by the acrylic.

Georges Vantongerloo

Instead of being concerned with planes made from flat sheets, Georges Vantongerloo's acrylic sculpture is linear. It consists of rods and cylinders twisted and bent into spiral shapes which either rest on a flat surface or spin on a wire from the ceiling. Vantongerloo started using transparent acrylic in the 1940's, late in his career, and he used it in a manner different from that of the other artists discussed here.

He seems to have been more interested in the potentialities of acrylic as a material than either Gabo or Moholy-Nagy. These men were primarily concerned with transparency, and they used glass and celluloid before acrylic became available. It almost seems as if Vantongerloo waited for acrylic to appear. It proved to be the perfect material for his experimental research with light and color.

The art historian Margit Staber made an interesting recent appraisal of him: "He had the sense of discovery and the newness of a world being constantly transformed by the developments of science and their application in technology. The future of an art adequate to these developments was for him only a matter of being able to find a medium which would make it possible to capture this state of change in a visible and tangible object of aesthetic value. Seemingly the abstract of abstractionists, he was in fact near to nature, trying to catch the laws which govern the appearance of things in space and time, and their impact on man."

Like Moholy-Nagy, Vantongerloo added touches of color to his first acrylic sculptures, painting them with dots and dashes. These constructions, most of them hand-size, seem to be a continuation of the ideas expressed in his wire sculpture of the preceding decade, except that he had begun to think as much of light and color as of space.

In 1960 Vantongerloo went to the Arctic Circle to see the aurora borealis. It impressed him greatly, and his last work is based on the spectrum. By using prismatic and cubic volumes of acrylic he created works that produce and alter their own coloration. He captured the color of light itself with these prismatic refractions. They are tangible ideas that have no association with traditional art, and he expressed them through what he referred to as "the incommensurable"; that is, the purely creative, indefinable, intangible spirit.

His main concern was the conception of a work; he had little interest in making "works of art," as commercial objects. This scientific spirit of research helps explain why he was satisfied with structures so small as to be only models for monumental work. When asked why he didn't execute his work on a larger scale he said there was no need to: the idea was there for everybody to see. He also pointed out that photography could bring out his intentions even better than the real thing because "the human eye would not yield to the planned effect." That is, the photograph did away with scale and allowed the viewer to "see" the sculpture in the size he desired. However, Max Bill says that Vantongerloo did have

plans of making objects on a monumental scale, and he and the artist had many discussions about executions, just before Vantongerloo died.

In his catalog for a Vantongerloo exhibition in London in 1962, Bill wrote, "He is completely in tune with the experimental thinking of our time, and his ideas are a characteristic expression of our age."

Georges Vantongerloo, "Coordonnées variables (Ondulatoires) points rouge, vert et violet" (1951; "Variable [undulating] coordinates: red, green, and violet points"), 15⅜" long. This linear work consists of thermoformed rods.

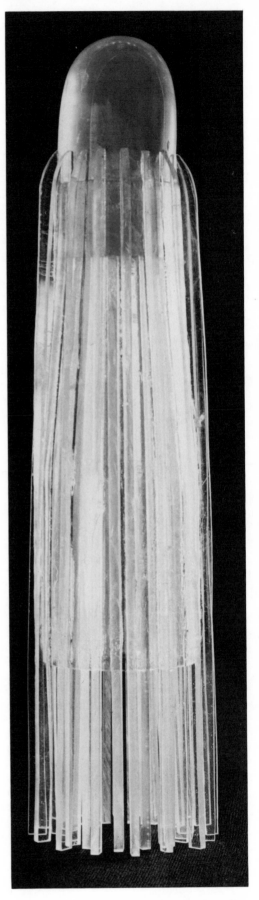

Georges Vantongerloo, "Comète" (1962; "Comet"), 11⅞" high. An oddly literal work from a man primarily concerned with abstract ideas.

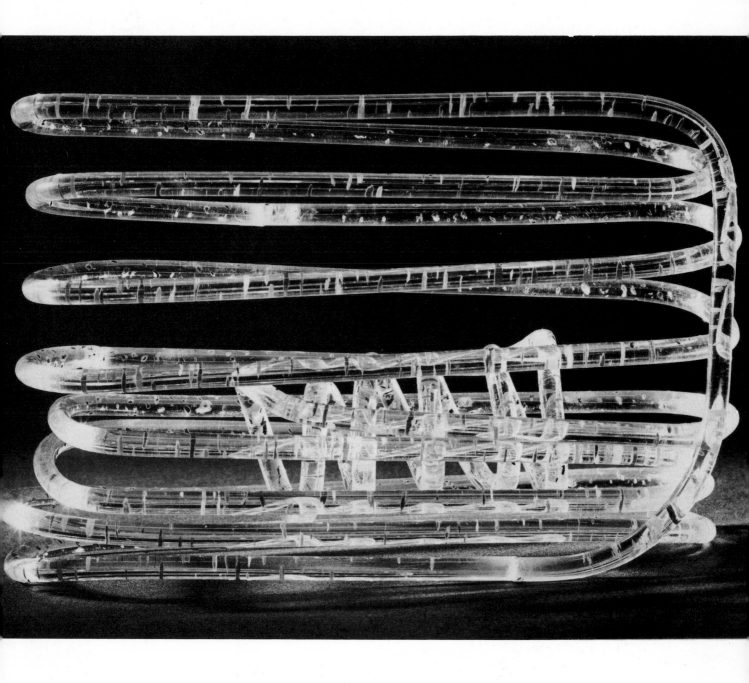

Georges Vantongerloo, "Segment d'espace" (1953; "Segment of space"),
8⅝" long. The second thermoformed rod inside the first counteracts the
main linear force, just as the spots of color on each rod are distorted
perpendicularly to the axis of the rod.

Xanti Schawinsky, "Cube" (1938). Schawinsky says no one knew how to work the material, nor were there facilities available at that time, so technicians at Rohm and Haas machined the sections to his specifications and delivered the work ready to be assembled, except for making the line incisions on the sides and shaping the center curved piece. To make this section Schawinsky built a wooden mold, then placed the cut and polished but straight and stiff sheet on the mold and thermoformed it to shape in a baker's oven.

Xanti Schawinsky, "Crystal" (1938). This was the three-dimensional section of a photomontage at the Pennsylvania Pavilion of the 1939 World's Fair. It was made of clear, gray-tinted acrylic sheets set in a 10 x 20" stainless-steel frame. The dark triangular sections were stainless-steel mirrors that reflected the outside environment, creating an ever shifting and expanding space. Walter Gropius and Marcel Breuer collaborated with Schawinsky on the photomontage.

Xanti Schawinsky

Xanti Schawinsky studied painting under Kandinsky and Klee and in 1924 joined the Bauhaus, where he later taught theater design. Like other Bauhaus artists, and in keeping with the Bauhaus idea of experimentation and exploration of materials and visual ideas, he worked in theater, ballet, architecture, and industrial and graphic design, using unconventional materials.

Looking at Schawinsky's work, one is struck by how readily he responded to new ideas and materials in art. Some of his paintings were done using an automobile as a brush substitute: he drove a car across large canvases, resulting in a maze of curved and intersecting tire tracks. For other paintings he fastened paint-soaked wooden blocks to his feet and danced on the canvas. It was the Gestalt which interested him: the record of an instant, the capturing of a fleeting movement. His technical knowledge allowed him to carry on other optical and kinetic experiments in stage presentations, in designs for expositions (such as those at the 1939 New York World's Fair), and with color and light.

In his art, Schawinsky worked out functional solutions to problems. He felt that the artist must forge a vital visual language rooted in the present. His art forms have intrinsic identification with the materials used, and he was antagonistic to techniques that result in alien images. The only honest way to approach art, he has claimed, is to start with a completely clear and uneducated consciousness, and then to evolve ideas through analysis and synthesis. Hence, art is not a matter of style but a knowledgeable and intuitive approach to a problem.

In his acrylic work *Cube*, done in 1938, Schawinsky anticipated much of what is happening in sculpture today. The minimal character of the sculpture and the visual illusion it created grew out of his concern with, and consideration of, the material. In effect, Schawinsky has been preoccupied with visual illusion throughout his career. He created a visual language which abolishes all emotional reference to become a communication of pure optics.

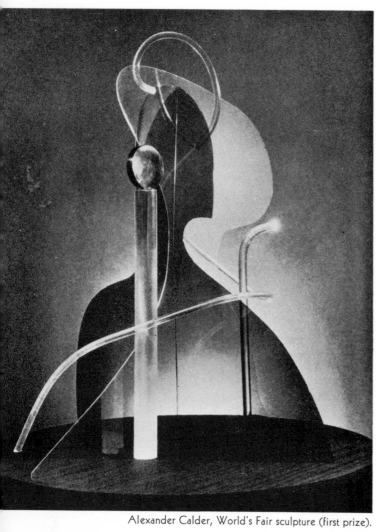

Alexander Calder, World's Fair sculpture (first prize).

Herbert Matter, World's Fair sculpture (second prize).

The 1939 World's Fair Competition

Schawinsky's *Cube* was done as a result of a World's Fair competition sponsored by the Museum of Modern Art and Rohm and Haas, the manufacturer of Plexiglas. The sculpture was awarded fifth prize and displayed in the Hall of Industrial Science, Chemicals, and Plastics, and later at MOMA.

Other artists who entered the competition included Alexander Calder, Herbert Matter, Werner Drewes, and C. K. Castaing. To the author's knowledge, however, only Calder, in one other piece, ever used the material again.

Calder's work won first prize in the competition, and he mentions it in his autobiography. His ideas about how to work the material did not jibe with the manufacturer's. "About this time, a Plexiglas manufacturer wanted to get some publicity, cheaply. So he put up a modest prize and published a lot of rules about what you could do with Plexiglas and how to work it. I entered this competition, but I did not like their suggestions on how to work it. I just used a hacksaw and a file. Anyway, they finally took my object and reproduced it— they thought—nice and smooth. Also, it turned out they did not have any black Plexiglas, and where I was to have vari-colored lights playing at the end of a two-inch stalk, they abandoned that as being too complicated, and made a horrible case for the thing, too.

"In spite of this, I was awarded the prize, because I knew the jury—or rather, the jury knew me."

The work as exhibited was edge-lighted by a concealed light in its base, and was constructed of sheets and rods of varying sizes and thicknesses. It included red, purple (a sub-stitute for the black Calder specified?), white, and clear acrylic.

In 1943, Calder constructed a small mobile, now in the study collection of the Museum of Modern Art, as a third-anniversary present for Yves Tanguy and his wife, Kay Sage. Written in French on the four parts of clear acrylic that make up the piece is "For three years of fairly good behavior." Very likely the piece was made of scraps left in his studio from the World's Fair piece.

Werner Drewes, World's Fair sculpture (third prize).

C. K. Castaing, World's Fair sculpture (fourth prize).

Contemporary artists using solid acrylic

Most of the early efforts using plastics, with a few exceptions, are tentative. Artists today are going beyond any parallel aesthetic with other media (notably glass) in their use of acrylic. It is only now that the material is being recognized for itself—for its inherent beauty and strength and not as a substitute material.

Today's artists are aware of the possibilities of the vast number of synthetic products available; and the general public is beginning to appreciate plastics as materials in themselves, containing aesthetic properties as valid as those of natural materials. We are beginning to realize the potential of plastic, and it has started to play a major role in twentieth-century sculpture.

An important aspect of the recent development in the use of plastic to make art has been the increasing emphasis on innovation. Another factor has been the availability of plastics that do not require industrial facilities but can be worked in the studio with ordinary wood tools. And generally speaking, the artist is usually alert to new philosophies, ideologies, and materials and techniques with which to express himself. Few artists today are removed from the influence of the technological society in which they live. Their experimental, and often chaotic, work is a reflection of the times.

Plastic has caused non-sculptors to venture into three-dimensional construction, possibly because of the way light affects it. Acrylic is so transparent that it does not seem to exist—yet, it is there even when it seems not to be. Thus it has an elusive and ambiguous quality that is in many respects in the province more of the painter than of the sculptor; it has already been pointed out that many acrylic sculptors began as painters. Direct confrontation with light is unavoidable when using clear acrylic, and light has always seemed to be a more vital concern to the painter than it has been to the sculptor. Perhaps the emotional nature of the painter is better able to relate to the flat acrylic sheet than to a more stubbornly three-dimensional material. The inflexibility of the "hunk" of matter that was traditionally the sculptor's raw material is now gone.

Clarence Bunch, assemblage of four pedestal sculptures on a mirror, as set up for the Director's Choice Community Gallery at the Brooklyn Museum in 1971.

Louise Nevelson

Louise Nevelson puts together what are essentially open boxes, one stacked on another. This method of working is Constructivist in nature and is ideally suited to acrylic. The plastic pieces she has done, although not stacked, give a visual impression of compartmentalization. She uses straight edges interspersed with contrasting quick curves that give her work the feel and look of efficiency; a 1930's idea of a diner, a sanitary lunchroom, or an automat. She joins the flat transparent pieces with metal screws and bolts that are plainly visible and become a part of the total aesthetic. The light penetrates and illuminates: an abstraction made concrete without the use of mass. "My total conscious search in life has been for a new seeing, a new image, a new insight," she has said.

Louise Nevelson, "Canada Series III" (1968), 42½ x 27 x 7½". The sealed box around the work serves to protect it both physically and visually, keeping the viewer at arm's length and creating a visual vacuum.

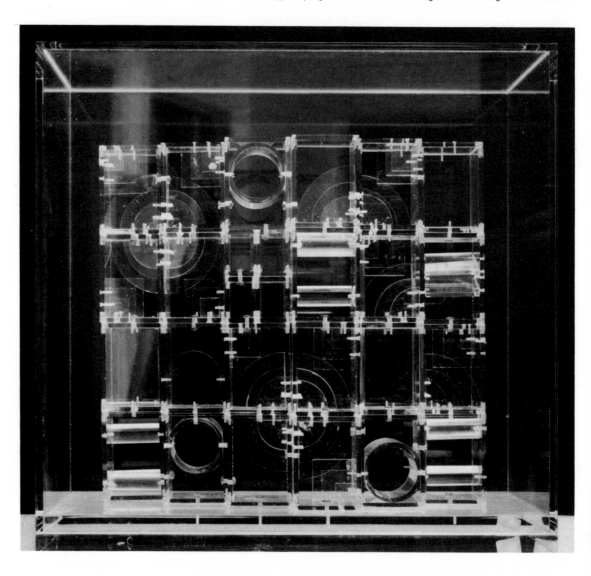

Louise Nevelson, ''Canada Series II'' (1968), 20 x 20 x 7½''.

Victor Pasmore

Art for Victor Pasmore is part of day-to-day life. His work is a reflection of an attitude which envisages art as a social, intellectual, and architectural phenomenon.

Pasmore believes that man must invent art. He cannot look to nature. He cannot "copy" and claim to have reinvented. To invent, the artist must create, with no reference to anything or any object that exists. The work must relate only to itself. "The search involves concentrating on the nature of objects and processes as 'things in themselves' whether they be a sheet of paper, a blot of color, the mark of a tool, the movement of the hand or the motion of a machine. By sensibility and concentration, we transform them. What matters is not what they can represent, but what they are 'existentially,' and what they can become. For my part escalation of visual reconstruction or symbolic representation was out of the question. What seemed to be required was not a new mirror or a new symbol, but a new process of development. Not a new model or a new idea, but a new 'essence' . . ."

Pasmore finds "existential essence" through working in a Constructivist manner. He builds logically, and the work becomes an organic whole—a real and integral part of the surroundings, as opposed to the picture-screen.

He believes the two-dimensionality of the picture plane is adequate only as an illusion, a kind of literary reference, and is not sufficient for twentieth-century needs. He found it necessary to use the actual scope of three dimensions and to build into space to achieve a dynamic relationship between the construction and its surroundings. He projects elements outward from a flat transparent plane, allowing the light to affect them as it changes during the day. The image changes with the mood of the hour, creating uncertainty as to what it is that we actually see.

In explaining the shift from his earlier lyric-romantic easel paintings to the objective architectural work, Pasmore states: "In the years immediately following the Second World War, I found myself faced with the necessity of attempting a fresh start. An analysis and reassessment of the various manifestations of the visual arts had left me in a state of confusion. I became conscious of the fact that if modern science had opened the door of the rigid frame in which classical art had contained the artist, it had left him groping in a new environment in which object was confused with subject, figure with background and individual with general. Freedom had been achieved, but at the expense of dehumanizing the image of man and denaturalizing that of nature. Furthermore, as if to reinforce this situation, the conflict between reason and instinct, fact and fantasy had come out into the open to split the imagery of naturalist art. Symbol and photograph vied with each other in a scramble for priority. Inner and outer world had become divided."

The scope of Pasmore's vision changed; he stopped painting and adopted the technical ideas of Constructivism and the use of machines to express light and space through relationships in actual dimensions.

His early reliefs of stone and painted plywood were related to the collages of a few years before and had a painterly, handmade quality. Since these did not give the space and light effects which preoccupied him, he turned to industrial materials—the hard, slick, reflective surfaces of acrylic as well as other synthetic materials—to express his ideas, and he replaced traditional illusionistic perspective by actual three-dimensional depth. The reliefs became more transparent and deeper, more active in space.

Pasmore's Constructivist work with acrylic and other synthetic materials and machine tools is concerned with dissociating elements like light, reflection, and transparency from the images that bring them to mind. The materials and tools leave an impersonal mark on the work that, although it seems a paradox, allows us to relate more intuitively to it. He is aware of the "essence" and not the "story." The work is no longer romantic, but objective and pure.

Victor Pasmore, construction (1965), 48 x 48 x 14". The piece protrudes from the wall, causing shadows which change under natural light during the course of a day.

Francisco Sobrino, "Espaces indéfinis SB2" ("Indefinite Spaces SB2," 1962-68), 76 x 16½ x 16½". The low-angle photograph suggests architectural constructions.

Francisco Sobrino, "Transposition A" (1965), 18 x 8 x 8". Again, a small piece photographed as architecture.

Francisco Sobrino

Architectural space and form characterize Francisco Sobrino's acrylic sculpture. The work is spacious and defies the environment as expansively as the wind defines open areas of the countryside. The pieces appear to be buildings of an unknown century—cool, aloof, and efficiently beautiful—while at the same time they are mystical, untouchable monuments from some past-future age. They reflect sunlight and rain and color the sky as one looks through the tinted sheets, changing it as a colored camera filter changes what is viewed through it.

Sobrino uses square planes of tinted transparent acrylic, letting the reflective and transparent nature of the material create optical diamonds and triangles. A square intersects another, producing visual shapes that do not exist in reality. Certain areas accept light, causing those surfaces to glow and reflect like a mirror; other areas accept light softly, letting one see through the panes to the planes behind. In this manner the work is constantly changing.

Francisco Sobrino, "Transformation Instable" ("Unstable Transformation," 1963), 200 x 90 x 90". The "unstable" aspect of the piece is not its painstaking joinery but the shifting visual illusions caused by the intersection of planes and their reflection of light.

Reginald Neal

Reginald Neal silkscreens patterns on clear or colored transparent sheets of acrylic, which he superimposes one over another to form three-dimensional boxes within boxes, sometimes enclosing objects of other materials. We look through the moiré patterns to the seemingly floating and dancing solid forms inside. He has created two patterns, two logical systems, that oppose one another to cause tension.

As the observer moves and keeps the work in view, the boxes unfold, each a multitude of visual impressions of line, color, and form interacting to define space and optical energy. This work is both object and image, rational and intuitive. The visual impact and complexity of feeling are somehow greater than the economical means seem to allow.

Reginald H. Neal, "12 Cubes Suspended" (1968), 12⅗₁₆ x 12⅗₁₆ x 14". The small cubes are wood, covered with copper-colored Mylar. They are mounted on plastic partitions, which have incised lines that glow with light and cast shadows. The piece rests on a mirrored base. Both photographs are positive prints and in both the piece is lit from the outside, but the different viewing points and lighting intensities produce very different effects.

Leroy Lamis

Only acrylic is used by Leroy Lamis in his work, which is made up of units of cubes and rectangles placed one within the other to create an illusion of rectangular solids. Lamis builds forms within forms, more often than not completely transparent, and creates enclosed spaces which, strangely enough, seem protected by the multiple layers of acrylic. These boxes, though pellucid, seem invulnerable, inaccessible, and mysterious.

Leroy Lamis, ''Construction #126'' (1967), 40½ x 8 x 8¼''.

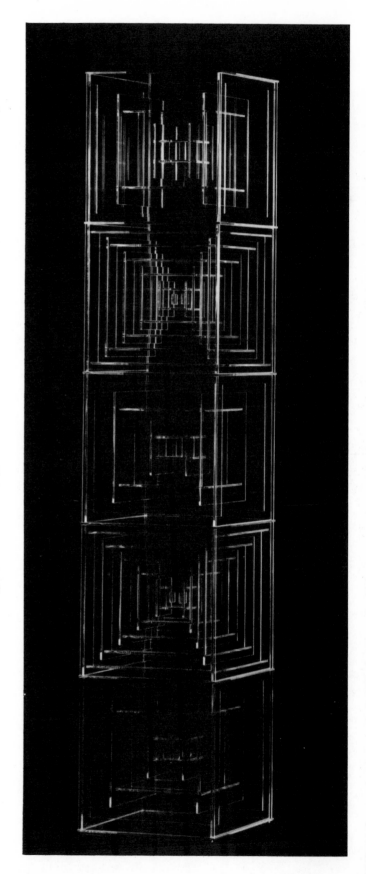

Leroy Lamis, ''Construction #150'' (1968), 22¼ x 6 x 6¼''.

Leroy Lamis, "Construction #136" (1967), 9 x 9 x 6¾". The piece
is made up of H-shaped units cemented together and enclosed
in a clear box.

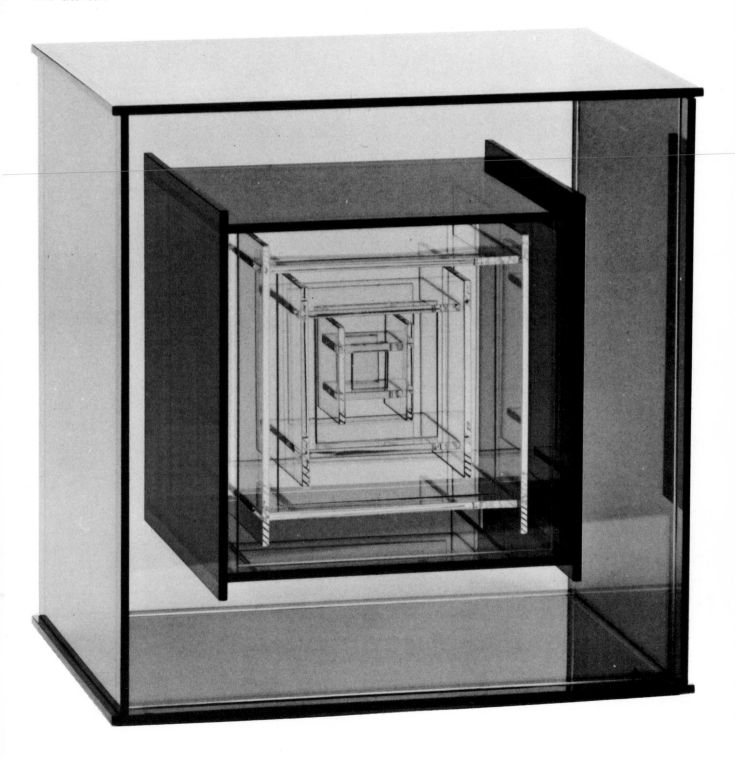

Charles Ross, "Broken Pyramid" (1968), 35 x 17½ x 17½". The two photographs show the same piece in different environments and with the parts placed in different relationships.

Charles Ross

Charles Ross makes huge, clear acrylic prisms filled with water or mineral oil. The prisms have their own special aesthetic based on optical distortion and an imposing surreal presence. The work has an inherent theatricality; it is an environment through which people move and see one another distorted and rainbow-hued.

The prisms have a curious way of outlining and rearranging objects and bending straight lines. The image is both inside and outside, and it alludes to something in the outside world. The pieces activate the environment in which they exist, yet, as objects, they are neuter—catalysts that contain little or no trace of the artist's personality.

Ross's concern is painterly—images are seen through, as it were, a window, and they are distorted and colored by manipulation of light passing through the prisms. He has chosen to work with these elements in three dimensions rather than on a flat plane, and an *Art News* critic claims: "Ross actually paints with light as aurora borealis effects appear at the edges of planes seen through the plastic. He demonstrated the extent to which sculpture can expropriate elements generally considered to be reserved for painting: the illusion of space and the manipulation of color, in this case broken light."

72CA1628

Sylvia Stone

At first glance, Sylvia Stone's flat, tinted, transparent, cut-out acrylic shapes seem to be solid and three-dimensional, but, in actuality, they are "two-dimensional" sculptures that exist on one plane. She achieves a kind of perverse perspective by painting a shape on the back of the acrylic sheet to suggest the receding plane of a cube. This produces an optical illusion of depth, implying a space-occupying character that the work does not possess. Stone then pulls the viewer up short again when he realizes that the perspective illusion of one end of the painted section may be denied by the shape of the opposite end. Each work stands clear, aloof, and strange.

Sylvia Stone, early sculptures. These are actually two-dimensional; the painted areas give an illusion of the third dimension.

Sylvia Stone, "Green Fall" (1969-70). Three sheets of pale-green acrylic create an actual distance between the forms rather than an illusion.

Craig Kauffmann, sculpture (1968), 43 x 89¼". It is thermoformed clear
acrylic with the inside surface spray-painted.

Craig Kauffmann

Craig Kauffmann makes wall "paintings" with a mysterious life of their own that has no relationship to the viewer. It is as if they were objects from space that exist in a vacuum, pulsating with life but not quite alive and articulate; and yet the work, which consists of unembellished, multiply produced objects, is formal. It is non-iconic, and at the same time it refers to more than itself.

The same motif, indeed the same vacuum-thermoforming mold, is used by Kauffmann to produce a series of acrylic sculptures in which the surface of each piece is treated alike. Or a series may consist of the same repeated shape with individual pieces colored differently. The repetition of differently colored shapes causes the work to vary enormously from one piece to another. Color becomes important independently of lineation. It is a separate entity and works in the same manner as in "color field" painting. The metallic color is applied by an industrial process to the inner surfaces. This situates the color deep within the orb so that it fluctuates before us rather than resting firmly on the surface. One looks *into* the painting-sculpture, not at it.

Kauffmann's work reflects a sophisticated treatment of the material itself rather than elements of configuration, and the work consists of simple, straightforward, nonelusive shapes that take on a presence and have mystery beyond the inert forms.

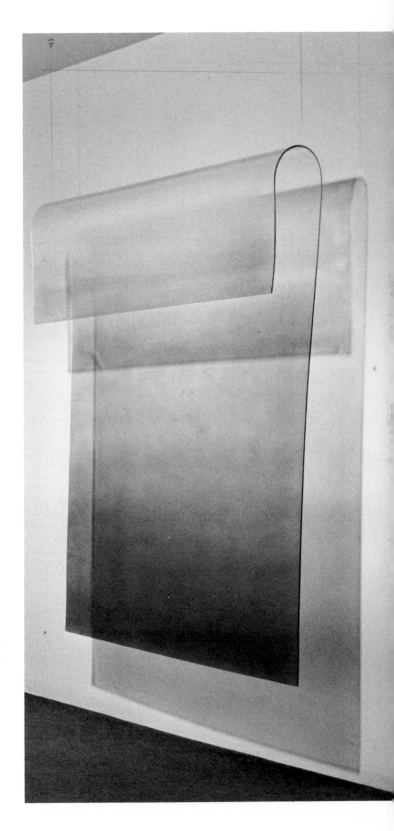

Craig Kauffman, wall sculpture (1969), 73 x 50 x 9".

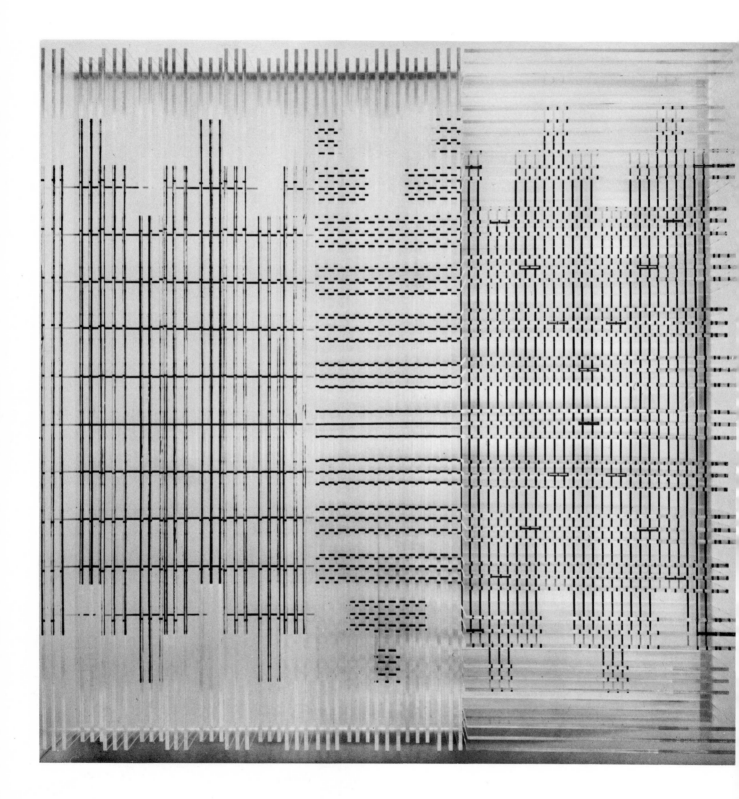

Mon Levinson

Electric light, paper and other opaque materials, and transparent acrylic are used by Mon Levinson in his geometric optical wall structures. His forte is relief work rather than sculpture in the round.

Shadow is an aesthetic concern of Levinson's, and he uses pieces of clear acrylic placed perpendicular to the background wall to cast shifting shadows as the viewer moves. The shadow work is pure in concept, simple and uncluttered. These pieces with their parallel lines are essentially Constructivist, though simplified and not as rhythmic as the work of Gabo or Pevsner. There are no curves and the straight movements are short and quick.

Levinson's light work employs small short rods of acrylic that protrude unevenly from the wall platform. They are only inches high and the tips are aglow from colored lights concealed in the base of the piece. Levinson takes advantage of the ability of the material to conduct light "like a pipe conducting water," as Archipenko put it.

Mon Levinson, "The Source V" (1970), 102 x 96 x 7". The incised grooves create a grid of shadows whose focus blurs as the distance from the light source increases.

Opposite:

Mon Levinson, "Stepped Shift I" (1968), 38" square. The work employs sheets rather than rods; the sheets are edge-lighted, and the edges are precisely colored with acrylic paint.

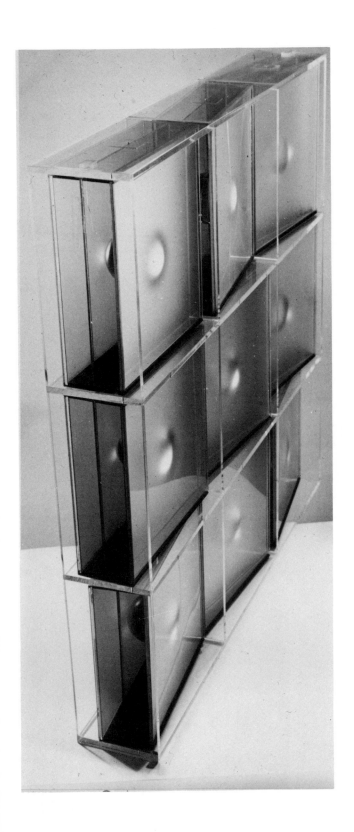

Leo Rabkin

Leo Rabkin is a painter whose enthusiasm for acrylic has made him a sculptor. He uses the frosted variety of solid acrylic in his light-and-movement sculpture, often incorporating small fans in the boxes so that objects will move and cast shadows on the translucent panes. The works of Rabkin create a fluid, shimmery fantasy world; occasionally mirrors capture the outside objective world—now distorted, multiplied many times, and made subjective.

Opposite:
Leo Rabkin, "Sea Sphere" (1970), 10" cube containing thermoformed green sphere.

Left:
Leo Rabkin, "Nine Moons." The units are identical, but each is positioned at a different angle.

William Reimann, hanging sculpture (1971). It is held together by a steel rod through the center, and square separators produce the arced forms—there is no thermoforming.

William Reimann, "Sphere" (1967). A steel rod holds the milky sheets together.

William Reimann

The ancestral spirit of Constructivism lies behind the elegant sculpture of William Reimann—elegant both in the visual sense and in the mathematical sense of economy and precision. Although dealing with mechanical smoothness, his work imparts a vibrancy directly related to nature and having little to do with primary structures or minimal art. The sculptured shapes come from ideas and fantasies triggered by experiencing change and growth in nature. The work is a direct response to the natural order of life expressed in an abstract idiom.

Reimann uses planes of translucent white acrylic, and each piece is precisely planned before execution. He initially shapes the pieces by clamping the sheets together in a solid and then grinding and carving until the final shape is achieved; then the individual elements are disassembled and reassembled many times and in many combinations until a statement of the experience and idea is arrived at. Then the piece is stabilized.

William Reimann, hanging sculpture (1971). This piece uses the same unusual technique as the piece on the opposite page.

William Reimann, model for outdoor sculpture commissioned by Harvard College Observatory (1971). A steel spiral supports the sections. The sculpture is planned to be 10 feet high.

Aleksandra Kasuba

Aleksandra Kasuba is intrigued with movement and space. She makes constructions of clear acrylic which are placed between a wall and a light mounted on a track that traverses slowly back and forth, producing moving linear shadows of the always static construction. A constantly changing space illusion is created. In this work the three-dimensional object itself has become secondary to the two-dimensional linear shadows as they exist momentarily on the wall-screen. Kasuba feels that "only motion has life," and wants her work to be "space-making rather than space-filling." A few years ago she turned from marble mosaic to acrylic in order to pursue this aesthetic idea.

Aleksandra Kasuba, wall sculpture. This piece depends on light, shadow, and movement for its effect. A light moves slowly back and forth at the sculpture's base.

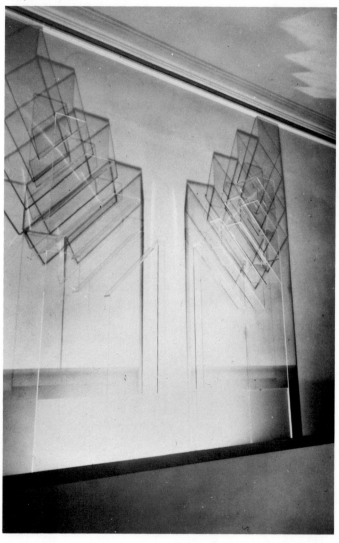

Aleksandra Kasuba, "The Queen," 96 x 60" including stand.

Gyula Kosice

Gyula Kosice uses clear acrylic to contain the flow of water and light. His sculptures confuse and play optically with the viewer; they are both relief and in-the-round. He creates ambiguity between water and light, so that the viewer mistakes one for the other. Sometimes he further complicates the situation by using movement in pieces he calls "hydro-mobiles."

Opposite, above:
Gyula Kosice, light-and-water sculpture (1970). It is four stories high. The projections are edge-lighted; water sprays against the hemispheres and falls to a basin below.

Gyula Kosice, hanging sculpture in a stop-motion photograph. The photograph approximates what happens in reality with acrylic; forms are reflected and multiplied.

SUMMARY

Artists working with acrylic today accept the material for what it is, for its inherent characteristics and natural beauty, rather than as a substitute for another material. They have found in acrylic a substance that allows expression of such intangible painterly concerns as light and space in three dimensions. Most of the contemporary artists whose work is discussed here were painters a few years ago—almost none were sculptors at the beginning of their careers. Many have not used other, more traditional materials in their work; they seem to have turned to sculpture and acrylic almost simultaneously. Yet it is they who have determined and defined the contemporary approach not only to acrylic, but to the sculptural ideas prevalent in the late 1960's and continuing on into the 1970's.

Painting and sculpture have become closer and closer both in material usage and in spirit, until it is difficult to draw a line between the two disciplines. The domain of today's artist may embrace elements of both painting and sculpture, which in turn may be combined with audience participation by forcing the viewer to move and react physically. Such involvement is an element of other contemporary art forms—happenings and environments. The artist also claims and incorporates elements of the dance as a peripheral sculptural means when he forces the spectator to become an active participant. The viewer's movements—his bending, twisting, and stepping forward and backward to see the piece properly—are dance traces.

Linda Levi, sculpture (1967), 14" diameter. The blowformed acrylic domes cover a polyester resin casting.

Opposite:

Neke Carson, "Moon-Man Fountain" (1968). This piece is conceived as a fountain in which people are the sculpture.

66

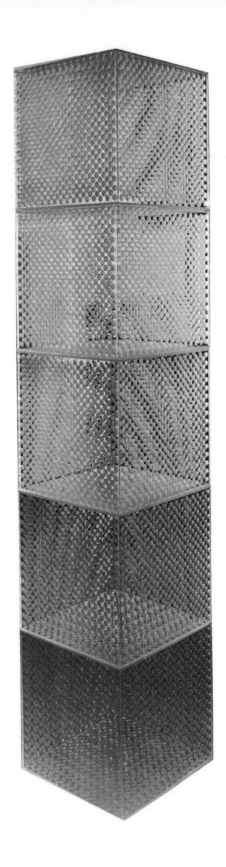

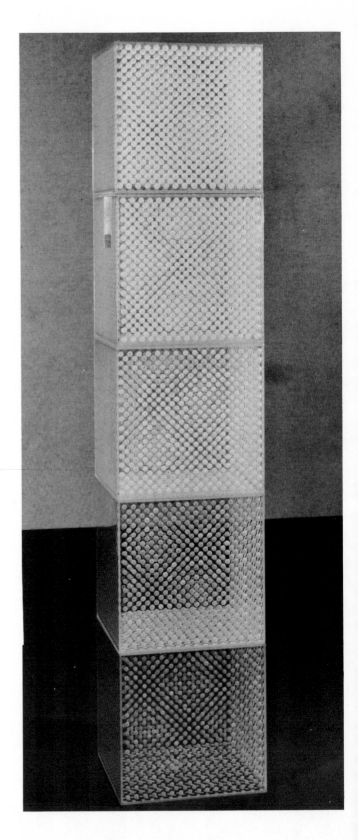

Clarence Bunch, column. It is made of multiple stacking units. The inside surfaces of the sheets that form each 16" cube have been routed to form a grid that creates moiré patterns as the viewer moves around the work.

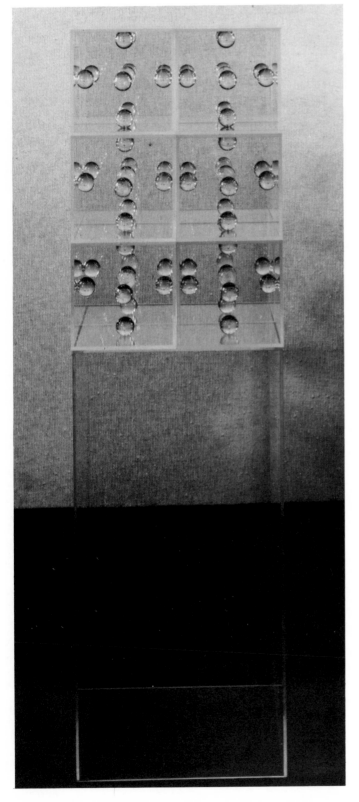

Other kinetic elements, such as flickering shadow movements projected on a wall or translucent screen, have been borrowed from the theater and the movies. Kinetics seem to be a natural element with acrylic (a "built-in" part of the material), whether the shadows move as in Kasuba's work, remain still as in Levinson's, or appear on screens as in Rabkin's.

Artists such as Moholy-Nagy projected and filmed shadows of acrylic structural forms for presentation as abstract movies. In such cases the acrylic sculpture becomes a means to an end. It ceases being sculpture in the ordinary definition of the word, because we are no longer directly concerned with the object itself, but with its shade. However, artists interested in mobiles use shadows directly in connection with the object, making the shadow play interact with the tangible sculptural form so that the shadow becomes a part of the aesthetic concern of the work.

With acrylic it is possible to create a kinetic still-object sculpture that does not in itself move but that contains movement activated by the viewer as he circles around looking at the piece. Neal's work functions in this manner.

Such movement in turn points up another intriguing factor of the material, its ambiguity. Although movement is present, nothing in the sculpture moves. Movement seems to be there, yet it is not. Indeed, the transparent material itself seems not to be present, yet it does exist solidly in three dimensions. It is not invisible, yet it seems to disappear. It is warm to the touch, yet it appears cold. The work becomes personal and subjective as one examines it, yet at first glance it is aloof and objective.

Most artists who work with acrylic approach the material from a Constructivistic viewpoint, and their work, by and large, has taken a boxlike form. Nevelson and Neal work in this manner, while other sculptors, such as Stone and Pasmore, prefer an optical illusion of three-dimensional forms that do not always actually exist.

Almost all acrylic sculpture is cool, aloof, introspective, in a strangely nonpersonal yet subjective way. The material seems objective, yet on close examination one sees more and more in it. It becomes richer with successive viewings.

Clarence Bunch, "Moonlight." The boxes can be rearrranged to suit the viewer.

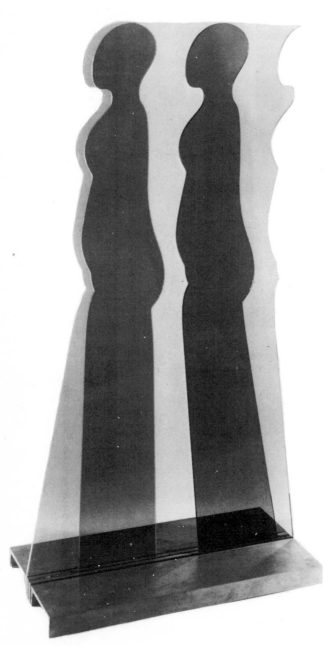

Susan Weil, sculpture, 44 x 22". The two figures are fluorescent red and yellow and are overlapped by a sheet of transparent blue, creating an orange and green glow on the figures.

Neal Small, "#0018" (1968), 6½ x 6½ x 18½". Solid acrylic forms are enclosed in a transparent box.

Charles Breed, "A Bokanovskified Egg Will Bud" (1968), 36 x 18 x 3". The piece is made of many layers of opaque and transparent acrylic shapes and is wired for sound, movement, and light.

Lillian H. Florsheim, sculpture. The work is composed of sliced cylinders.

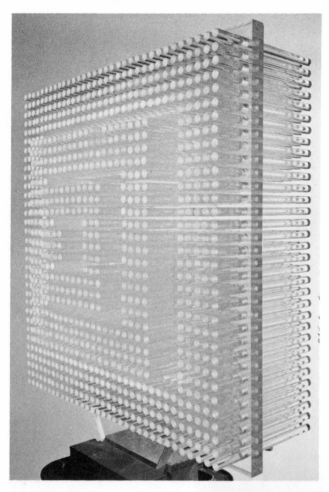

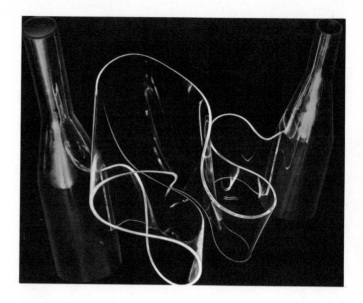

Above:
François Dallegret, sculpture (1967). The piece is made of a rippling thermoformed sheet of acrylic secured at each end by a tapered aluminum "bottle," one of which contains a fluorescent fixture to edge-light the piece.

Left:
Lillian H. Florsheim, sculpture. The artist's technique is unusual; most often acrylic sculpture is enclosed, taking the form of boxes, but this work is open to the surrounding environment. Hundreds of solid rods pierce a single thick sheet of acrylic.

Doris Chase, "Nesting Forms." The five separate forms were sawn from a thick piece of acrylic, and the edges were left unpolished.

Ruth Vollmer, "Tangents" (1970), each piece 18" high. The work is concerned with and illustrates a geometric principle: convex surfaces whose width is constant can be rotated between two fixed parallel plates to which they remain tangent.

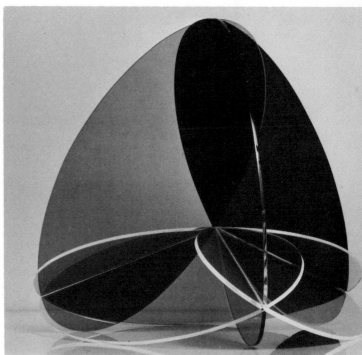

Ruth Vollmer, "Intersecting Ovals" (1970), 12 x 12 x 12". Each of the six ovals of different-colored transparent acrylic meets the other five at a central point, illustrating another mathematical principle, the so-called Steiner Surface.

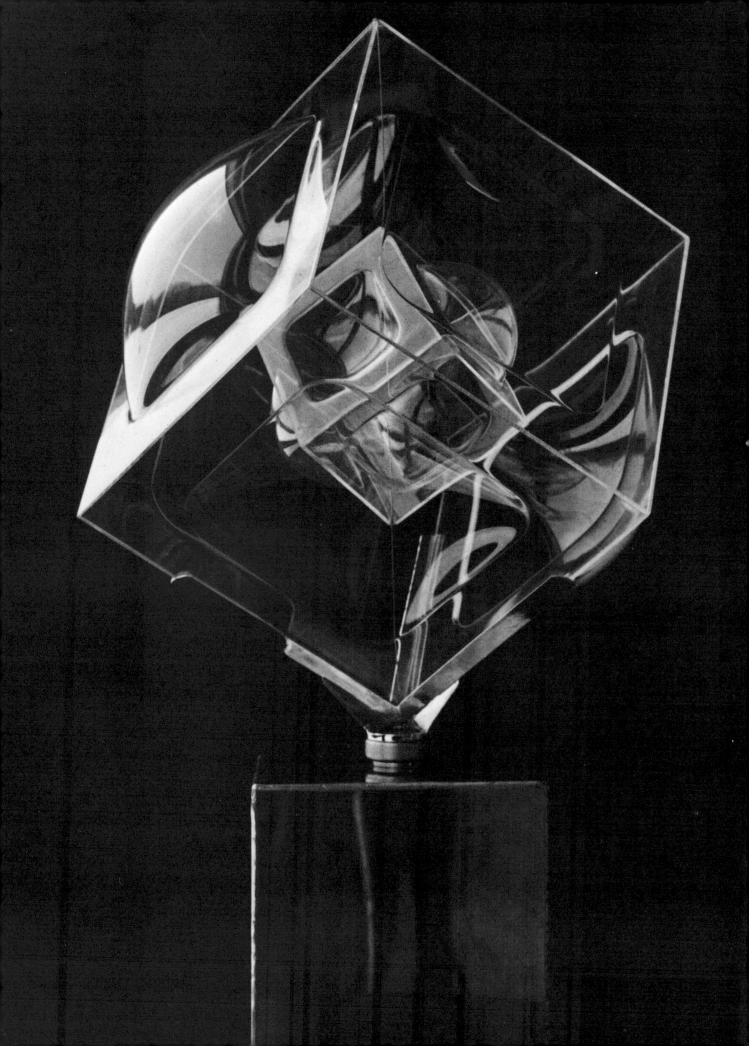

Aaronel deRoy Gruber, "The Space Within" (1969), 6″ cube inside 18″ cube. The bulges in the cubes were made by thermoforming. The base is motorized.

Right:

Feliciano Bejar, group of "Magiscopes" in the artist's studio. Lenses of acrylic are set in metal frames.

John Chamberlain, sculpture, 24 x 55 x 44″. Chamberlain heats acrylic boxes and reshapes them, revealing the grace and fluidity inherent in the material.

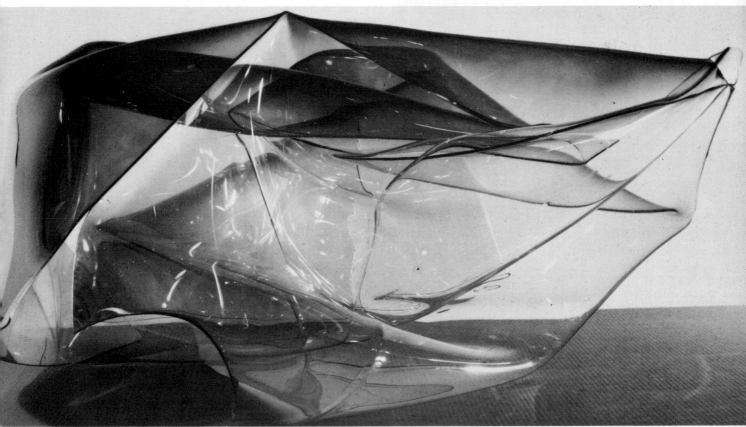

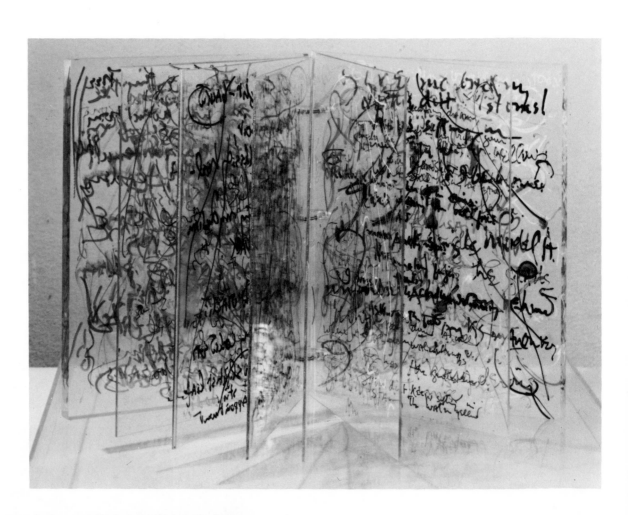

Above:
Elise Asher, "The Testing Tree" (1970). The sculpture is in the form of a book with painted calligraphy that is, in the author's words, "neither wholly decipherable nor entirely undecipherable." For a text she uses the works of her husband, the poet Stanley Kunitz.

Left:
Eduardo Ramirez, "Topological Construction (White)," 24 x 43 x 16". Made of opaque white sheet.

Opposite:
Rogelio Polesello, column (1970), 48 x 25 x 25". The circles were routed and carved, then highly polished.

Babette Newburger, chair and nesting stools.

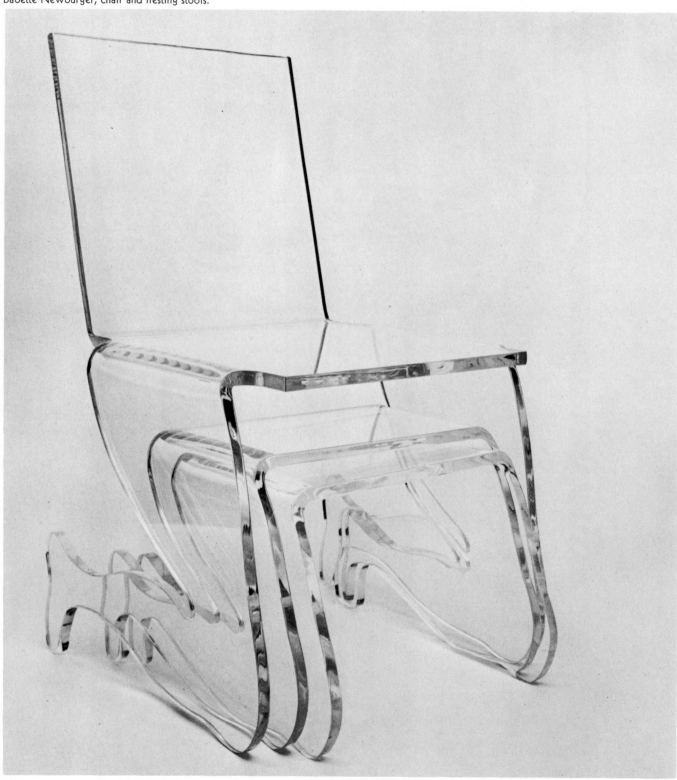

3.
ACRYLIC FURNITURE
AND JEWELRY

Lamps and chairs seem to be the most popular furniture items produced using acrylic. Lighting devices are a natural use because of the material's clarity, light-transmitting ability, and thermoforming possibilities. It is harder to understand acrylic's ready acceptance in other furniture construction. After all, it scratches easily and is difficult to keep clean because it attracts dust through static electricity; and although strong and not likely to break under ordinary strain, it does bend and "give" under weight so a chair never seems quite solid and stable to the person seated.

However, aesthetically speaking, acrylic furniture is successful, sometimes spectacularly so. Most furniture designers use clear transparent acrylic in their work, which changes the ambience and visual relationship of an interior, creating a glitter and a great sense of space where very little may exist. It sometimes has a startling effect in changing the environment.

Babette Newburger is perhaps not so much a furniture designer as a sculptor whose works masquerade as furniture. But her technical skill and originality, and her sense of humor, are all too rare in the field of furniture and jewelry design, so I have used her pieces as an exemplary beginning for this chapter.

The lines in her work are clean, energetic yet relaxed, and witty. The three-quarter-inch sheets she prefers to work with provide both visual and physical strength and stability. The pieces shown here are of transparent acrylic, but she sometimes uses green, blue, and yellow—not only for the color, but to conceal variations in the material as it comes from the factory; clear uncolored sheets from different batches may vary in clarity and thickness and be difficult to match.

Mrs. Newburger feels that acrylic is a tremendously flexible substance that the public is just beginning to explore; its aesthetic and functional roles in our lives are yet to merge. At the present she considers much design work using acrylic to be cheap-looking and novelty-oriented—even when the items are done by competent artist-designers. But a few people have shown a natural inclination and feel for the material. She herself has been experimenting with it in many directions: she has made a thirty-foot mobile on an exterior wall in Spain and has also made belts and headgear, and she is working on a bathroom unit that will recycle water.

Babette Newburger, telephone. It works.

Babette Newburger, table. The legs are modular units and can be arranged in various provocative positions. It is something more than furniture—perhaps a huge toy—and yet it is a serviceable table. Compare her bathtub illustrated later in this chapter.

Jacques Famery's "Kaleidoscope" armchair is like a transparent butterfly. Its curves undulate, swoop up, down, around, toward one, and then away in movements like music and dance. His work has moved from traditional chair shapes used by most designers to an imaginative form for the future. He has given us a new way to view, and to think about, a chair. This structure is possible because of the thermoforming capabilities of acrylic. These exciting curved, fluid forms would not be practical in other materials. Indeed, it would not be possible to achieve the same aesthetic sensation with any material other than acrylic.

Jacques Famery, "Kaleidoscope" armchair.

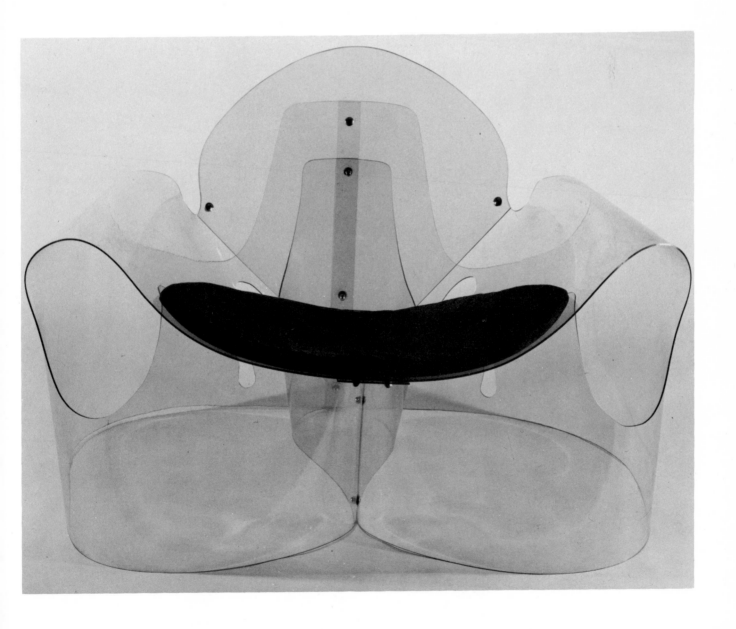

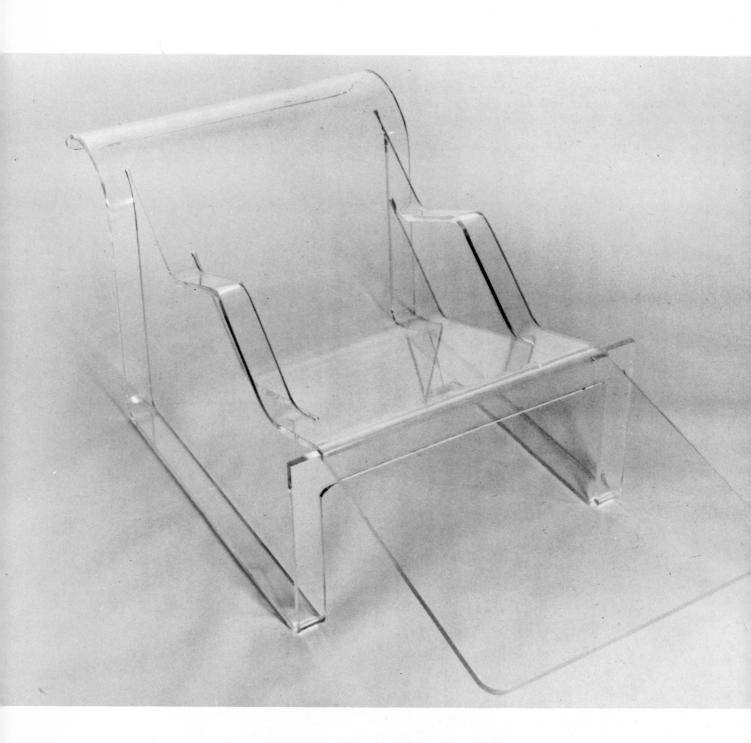

John Mascheroni, chaise longue.

John Mascheroni's beautiful crystal-clear furniture, each piece constructed of a single sheet of acrylic, is thermoformed into well-proportioned bar chairs, a classic chaise lounge, tables, and pedestals to be used for plants or to display sculpture and other objects. His upholstered armchair and ottoman is a simple and efficient design that seems to float and hover above the floor. These designs accommodate the material well both aesthetically and structurally, and in their simplicity and economy of means approach sculpture. There are no tricks here—just a straightforward approach and honest use of the material.

John Mascheroni, bar chair.

John Mascheroni, upholstered armchair and ottoman.

In contrast, another designer's upholstered chair, although pleasing in its conventional simplicity, seems to use acrylic not for itself but as a substitute for some other material, possibly wood. The chair does not give testimony to new thought; our consciousness is not expanded by it aesthetically, nor are we stimulated intellectually. Wood would have been more pleasing visually and much more sturdy.

Left:
John Mascheroni, pedestal table. The top is not acrylic but glass. Mascheroni makes similar pedestals in other proportions.

This upholstered chair is not as successful as Mascheroni's furniture.

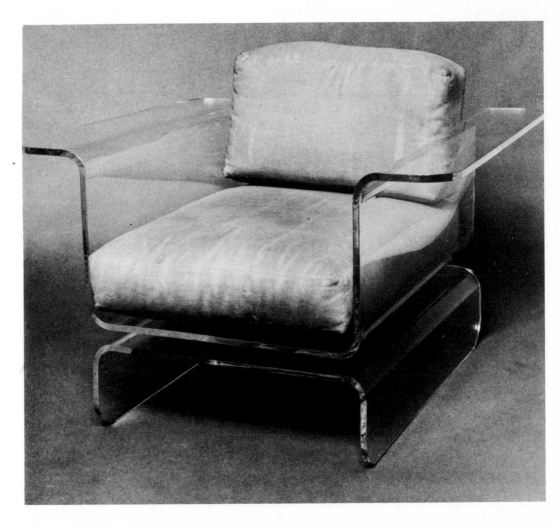

Spiros Zakas's chair of a single sheet of clear acrylic bends gracefully where the spine touches, where the knees bend, and at the base. It is a simple silhouette with a naked sexy look. His furniture has a soft rounded quality. His magazine table has a substantial, almost bulky feel, yet it too is constructed of a single piece of clear acrylic.

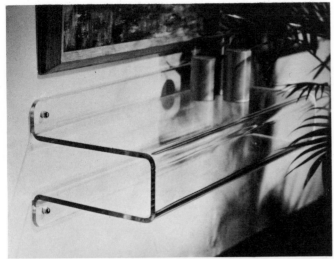

Left:
Spiros Zakas, wall shelf.

Spiros Zakas, chair.

Opposite:
Spiros Zakas, magazine table.

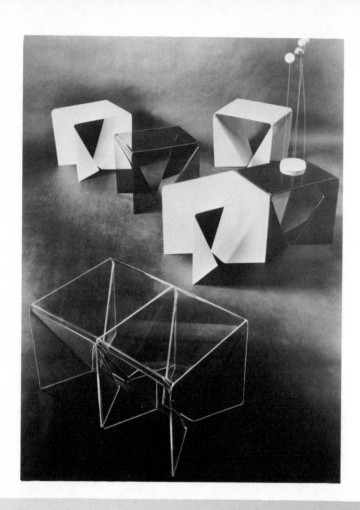

On the other hand, Neal Small's chair and occasional table (also of one piece of clear or colored transparent acrylic) are sharp, angular, and quick in movement. His ice-bucket tables are amusing novelties that would not be possible in any other material. The same is true of Babette Newburger's beautiful tongue-in-cheek full-sized bath tub.

Small makes beautiful lamps of clear, translucent, and opaque acrylic. Some of his small table lamps have a look and feel of the 1930's.

Left:
Neal Small, occasional tables. These are available in various transparent and opaque colors as well as clear.

Babette Newburger, bathtub (1968), 19 x 60 x 30". The tub is blow-formed, and the legs are hand-carved.

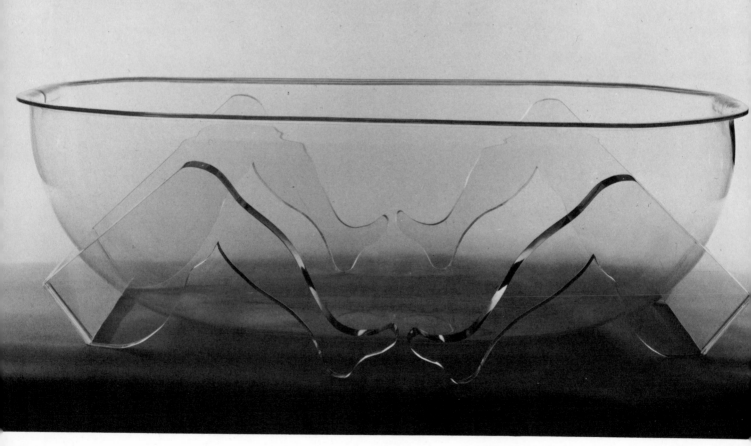

Left:
Neal Small, table lamps.

Neal Small, ice-bucket tables.

Ugo La Pietra's clear bubble lamp with textured surface is sculpture that happens incidentally to function as a lamp.

Edward Sheats' lamp of clear and opaque acrylic, which can be hung from the ceiling or rest on a table, is completely different from La Pietra's. It uses planes and angles rather than spheres and circles.

Ugo La Pietra, "Globo Tissurato" lamp, 28" high. The bulb is clearly visible, becoming an aesthetic part as well as a practical physical part of the work.

Opposite:

Edward J. Sheats, lamp.

91

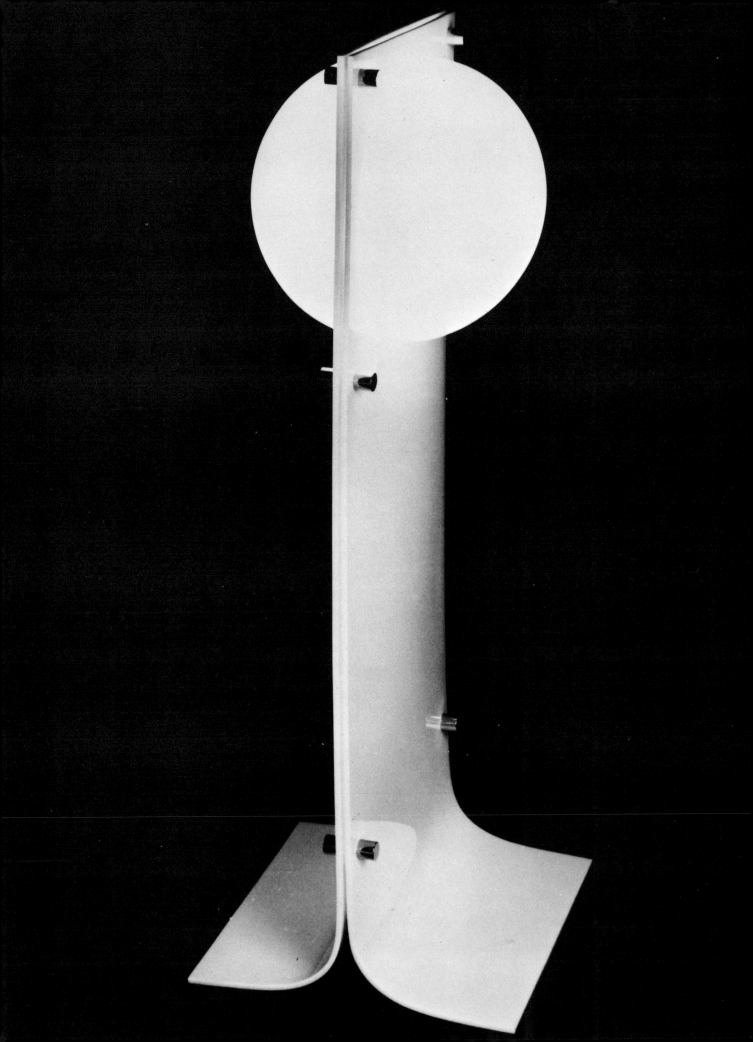

Opposite:
Neal Small, floor lamp.

Babette Newburger, lamp.

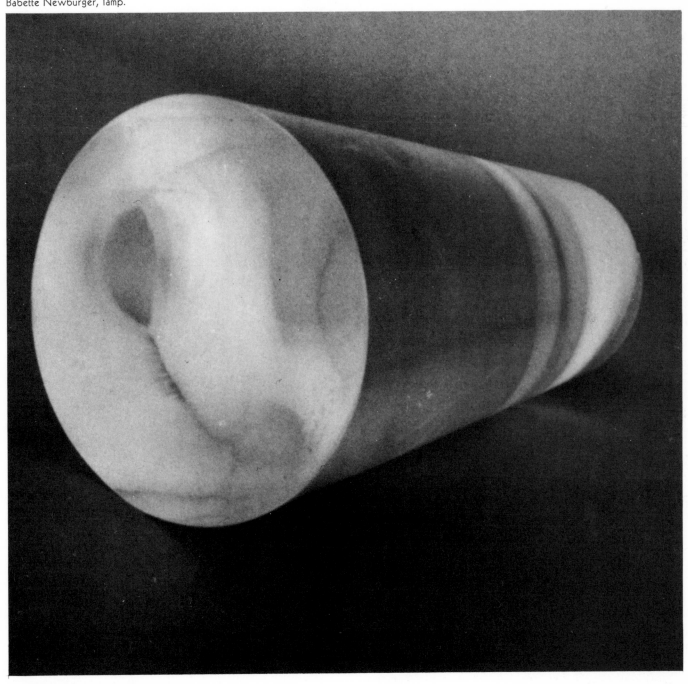

Andrew Morrison, magazine table.

Andrew Morrison's single-piece table and magazine rack is a handsome and utilitarian object in opaque colored acrylic.

Dining on Terrence Cashen's table and sitting on his chairs would be like living in the twenty-fifth century. They have an other-world look about them.

Terrence Cashen, table and chairs.

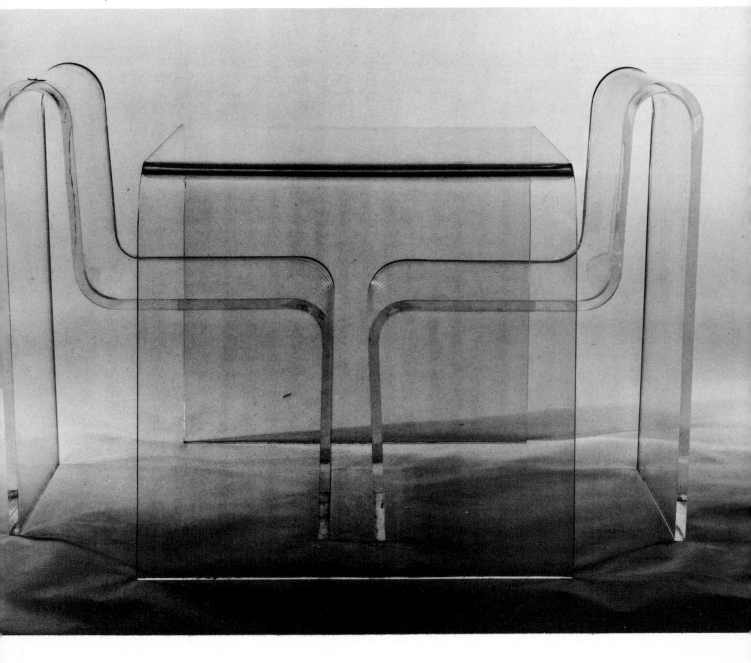

Richard Abbott's chaise-longue-and-table combination of milk-white opaque acrylic works because of its extreme simplicity, almost starkness. His small chair of the same material and color is like Christmas ribbon candy. It has a warm and amusing springy quality that is distinctly human. Abbott's commercial displays use the same open sweeping curved lines he employs in his furniture designs. Here also he seems partial to white opaque acrylic.

Richard Abbott, armchair.

Richard Abbott, chaise-longue-and-table.

Richard Abbott, commercial display.

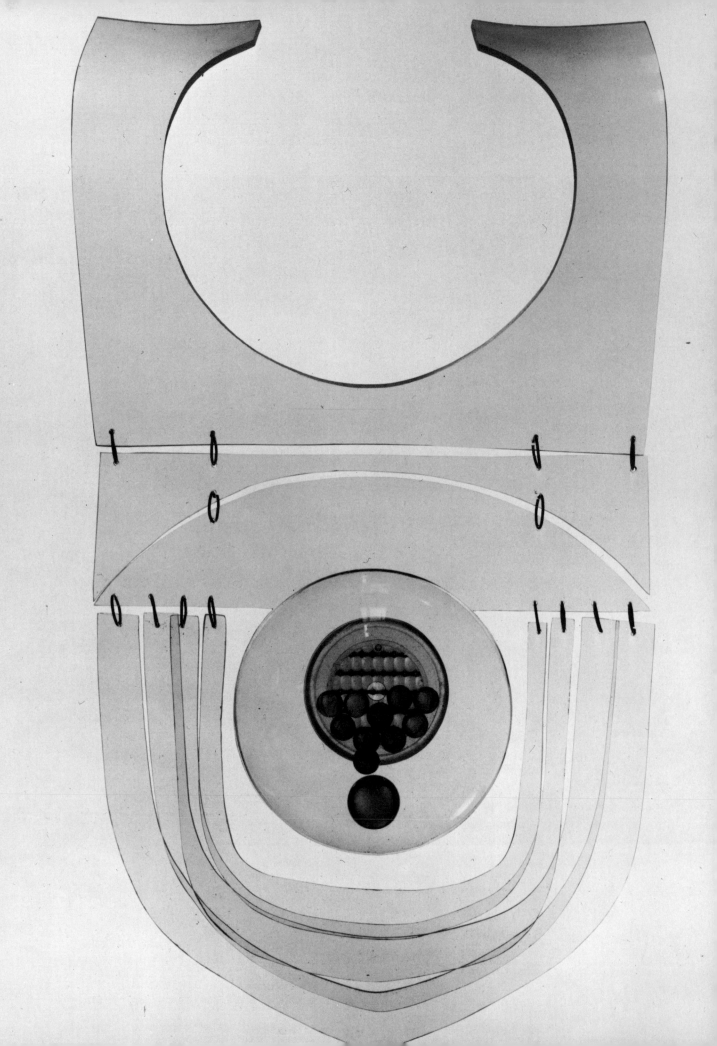

JEWELRY

Acrylic is a natural material to use for jewelry. It is brilliant as diamond and uses light to good advantage in small objects such as rings. The movement of the body intensifies its sparkle and glitter.

However, with a few extremely exciting exceptions, the acrylic jewelry that has appeared up to now has been novelty stuff. Component parts can be bought and put together quite easily and simply by anyone, and as a result, there is a rash of acrylic jewelry on the market—much of it with no value as far as design quality and use of material are concerned. But fortunately a few designers are working with acrylic in a serious manner.

Sculptural concerns make themselves felt in Carolyn Kriegman's jewelry. Her necklace-collar is historic in feeling, reminding one of the grandeur of royalty, of Egyptian princesses.

Carolyn Kriegman, neckpiece, 8 x 14". The rounded center forms are colored acrylic; each shape acts as a lens.

Bix Lye's rings are like machinery, cogs and wheels. They are bulky and have incised ridges. They are mostly of clear transparent acrylic with touches of color added.

The curved fluid lines of Michael Singer's bracelet suggest the serpentine forms of ancient jewelry. Acrylic gives the fluorescent piece a spring and vitality.

Bix Lye, rings.

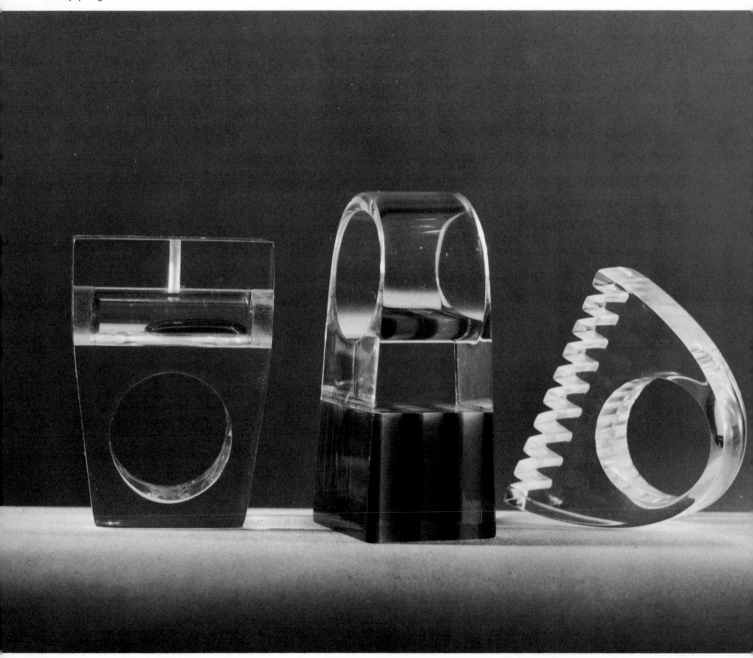

Michael Singer, bracelet.

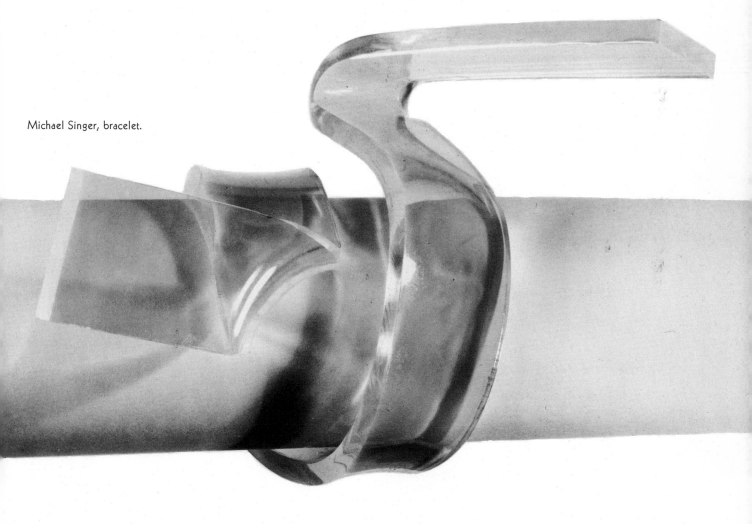

Michael Rhodes's jewelry has a serene, contemplative, straightforward, no-nonsense look. But at the same time the work has a substance and mass that is unusual in jewelry, or in acrylic for that matter. As delightful as it is, and as much fun as it affords, it is serious and innovative in the best sense of the words. The outsized earrings that fit the front of the ear rather than being affixed to the ear lobe show an approach that is valid and has not been explored to any extent. It is simultaneously humorous and serious in its wittiness, a brilliant and beautiful conception.

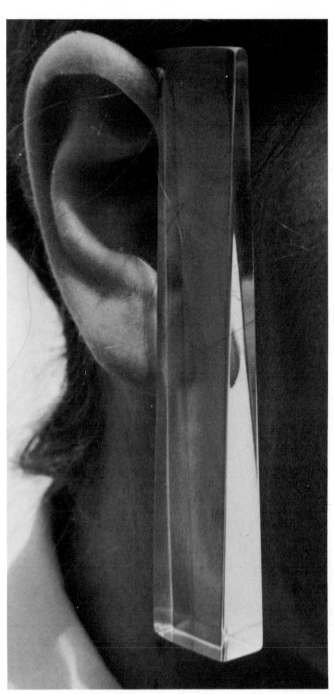

Michael Rhodes, earrings.

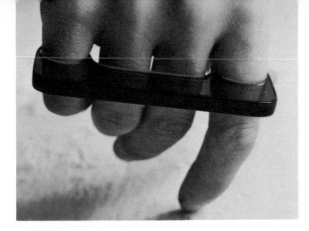

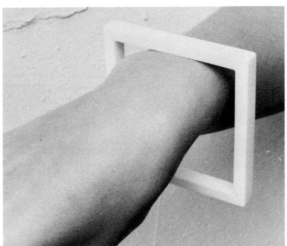

Rhodes's transparent brown two-finger rings in their deliberate awkwardness recall the brass knuckles of the prohibition era. Much of Rhodes's work is reminiscent and nostalgic.

The square and semicircular bracelets are shapes that oppose the body, and they work beautifully because of this opposition. It seems to be the ambiguity that interests Rhodes; contradictions give a presence to his work.

Michael Rhodes, bracelets, two-finger ring.

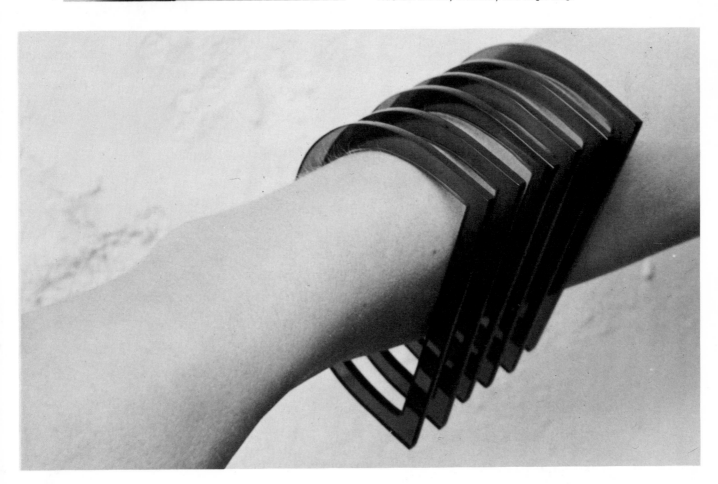

Spheres of different sizes seem to float on Vince Pasacane's acrylic collar. Each magnifies and reflects the others, creating a quick blinking movement within its stillness. At the same time the spheres are like soap bubbles clustered at the throat. It is a kind of out-of-space ornament that one might wear on Venus, or see in a Buck Rogers comic strip.

Vince Pasacane, neckpiece.

Ellen Dimsdale, pendant.

4.
WORKING WITH SOLID ACRYLIC

Acrylic can be hand-worked and machined in the same general manner as wood and metal. It can be sawed, cut, turned, routed, drilled, bent, and subjected to a host of other fabrication techniques, with hand tools like those used for wood and metal. It can, of course, be bonded. It can also be thermoformed, and many of the thermoforming processes are quite simple.

Solid acrylic lends itself readily to experimentation with no tools at all. A great deal of work is a result of manipulating pre-cut pieces of the material. Forms manufactured for a specific industrial purpose are often used by the artist for his own ends.

A well-stocked plastic supply store will carry acrylic in many sizes of sheets and in other shapes such as cylinders, rods, spheres, and cubes.

Probably the simplest way to go about working the material is to assemble ready-made parts. Some artists use acrylic ball bearings as elements in sculpture that act as lenses, magnifying and distorting images and playing with light. Also there are many small boxes on the market that when combined one with another or filled with other acrylic forms or non-acrylic materials make fascinating paperweights and hand sculptures—small pieces that can be fondled and played with. Unusual colors can be created in this manner by encasing one colored box inside a box of another color. These can be used alone or in combination.

Stacking is a useful technique because of the limitations of size and weight when transporting acrylic sculpture. Also stacking multiple objects of acrylic creates an infinity-like image that is not possible with other materials. Stacking and rearranging various acrylic shapes offers a quick ready outlet for creative activity, and the pieces can be used over and over again to create different objects, much as a child plays with blocks.

Acrylic spheres seem like sculptures in themselves, just as they come from the manufacturer. They invite incorporation into assemblages of ready-made parts.

When acrylic sheet comes from the manufacturer, it is covered with a protective masking paper. In order to avoid scratching the surface or chipping the edges of the sheet, the operator should leave the paper intact during all machine operations. If for some reason the protective paper is removed, the acrylic to be machined should be re-covered with masking tape or some other material.

Tools with tungsten-carbide-tipped teeth are preferred for cutting acrylic, because they are more wear-resistant, retain their sharpness longer, and cut faster and cleaner, thereby providing better machined finishes than ordinary wood or metal tools. Tools tipped with tungsten carbide must be kept sharp, with all knicks and burrs eliminated from the cutting edges. A good machine cut lessens other machine and hand finishing and polishing chores.

Dull wood- or metal-working tools have more of a scraping action than do sharp tools; for this reason they are less likely to chip the edges of the acrylic, and they produce reasonably satisfactory cutting results. However, most wood- or metal-cutting tools do not cut as cleanly, or as easily, as those tipped with tungsten carbide. The operator should be cautioned that tooling with dull and improper equipment may build up internal stresses within acrylic that will become apparent as crazing, or a cracking of the surface, long after the piece of work is completed. However, annealing (heating the machined piece to near its forming temperature) will help prevent crazing.

Cleanliness is very important when working with solid acrylic plastic. A small hand vacuum cleaner can be used to remove sawdust, dirt, and chips from the working area. Such debris can scratch the surface of the acrylic, sometimes even through the protective masking paper.

Any smooth surface that is easy to clean will provide a satisfactory working area, and a plain woven cotton fabric covering lessens the possibility of scratching the acrylic.

Acrylic sheet is protected on both sides with masking paper. Leave the paper on as long as possible.

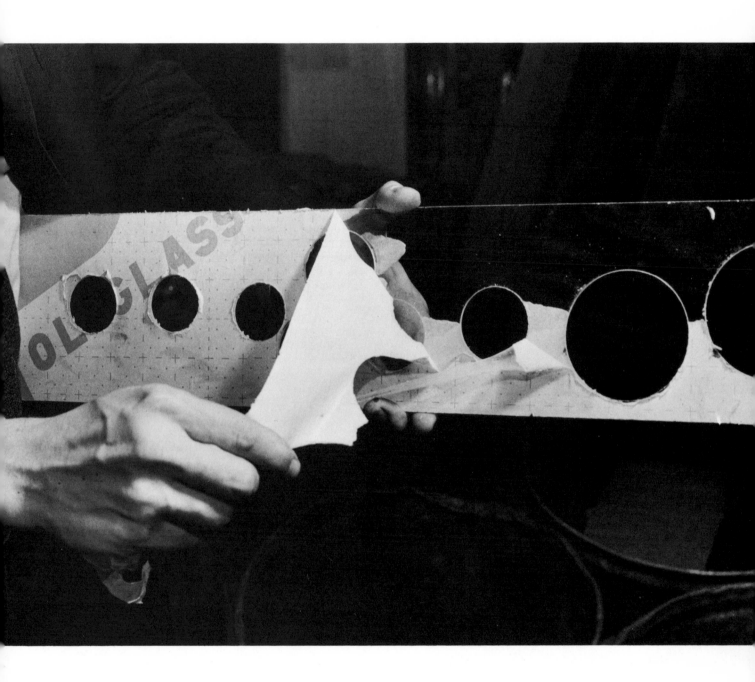

SAWING & CUTTING

The choice of saws and kinds of blades depends on the type of acrylic to be cut, the thickness of the sheet, and the kind of cut to be made. This will be explained below.

The operator must feed the material cautiously, slowly, and steadily, in order to prevent overheating, which causes acrylic sawdust to melt, accumulate on the blade, and obstruct the cut. The work must not be forced, and the teeth must be cleaned often for best results and to assure greater safety.

The sheet to be cut should be firmly clamped, both for safety reasons and to help prevent chipping. During the cutting operation, the blade should be rigid to prevent cramping, because a cramped blade can also result in a chipped surface.

The use of a coolant such as water or a lightweight oil will help dissipate frictional heat, extend blade life, and reduce the tendency of acrylic to melt and accumulate, or "gum up," along the edge of the blade. However, a coolant is not necessary unless the acrylic is exceptionally thick or the saw speed extremely fast.

Circular Saws

Circular saws are preferred for making straight cuts. The blade should be at least eight inches in diameter and hollow-ground to aid cooling and to help prevent binding. The sawteeth should have no rake, be the same shape, and be of uniform height. Thin "square and advance" teeth diamond-ground to close tolerance and with alternate teeth to start and finish the cut are preferred. Blades can be obtained from retail outlets or they may be made to specification by a tool manufacturer.

Working procedure is not radically different from working with wood. The height of the sawblade above the table should be slightly greater than the thickness of the sheet to be cut. The operator should, as with wood, hold the work firmly and tightly to the guide bar, which, of course, forces the acrylic in a line parallel to the saw blade. The speed of the feed should be reduced as the cut is started and when the sawing is nearly completed to avoid chipping corners of the sheet. The thicker the acrylic, the slower the speed of the saw should be, to protect the sheet against overheating. If the material is too thick, or if the speed of the saw is too high in proportion to the feed, the increase in friction will cause the acrylic sawdust to melt and accumulate in the recesses of the blade teeth.

A straight-line cut with a circular saw. One quickly learns the proper saw speed and pressure to prevent binding and melting.

Band saws

The band saw is an unusually versatile tool. It can cut straight lines but is particularly suited to cutting curves of moderate radius and executing complex configurations, provided an extremely narrow blade is used.

A good blade for general use is three-eighths of an inch wide, measured from the apex of the teeth to the blank, or back, side of the blade, with ten to fifteen teeth per inch.

To avoid obstructing and possibly breaking the blade, the operator should not bind the blade by trying to force the saw to accept the sheet faster than the blade cuts. A firm and steady but not rigid feed is essential.

There is a tendency for the fresh band-saw cut to reknit behind the blade more than with a circular saw. Because of the shape of the teeth on the saw blade and the operational speed of the saw, the heat-friction problem is aggravated, and so it is necessary to use a coolant with this tool. A solid lubricant, such as a bar of soap, will act as a coolant and prove more convenient and less messy than oil or water.

The operator will find that a band saw with a deep throat will allow for flexibility in his work. Not only can he use larger pieces of acrylic than with a narrow-throated saw, but he will find that such a machine provides for greater maneuverability and ease of operation.

Jig saws

For interior cuts and small-radius curves, a jig saw is an essential tool; indeed, it is the only tool designed to accomplish complicated interior cuts. The narrow blade must have a variegated-tooth, or "skip-tooth," structure, and be of the metal-cutting variety. Such a blade can easily be inserted through a hole drilled in the acrylic. The jig saw cuts well through extremely thin plastic, but the stroke of the blade is so short that the blade does not have a chance to clear the chips, which can melt and cause gumming with thicker sheets. When this occurs, the melted acrylic may reknit and fuse around the blade.

The jig saw is useful for complicated cuts in thin sheets.

Hand saws

Hand saws that are suitable for cutting acrylic include the coping, fret, and finer-toothed hack saws. Rip saws and large-toothed crosscut saws are too coarse and sometimes uneven, causing chipping. A fret saw or a jeweler's saw is the most satisfactory hand-operated cutting tool, since a greater range of tooth sizes is available. The limitations of the fret saw, however, are obvious; its size and method of use limit the size of the sheet that can be tooled.

Other cutting devices

Cutting devices such as electric knives and electrically heated wires, if used at all, must be employed with extreme caution, since they may prove to be fire and safety hazards. Other cutting tools—snips, shears, knives, and score cutters—have such limited efficiency in cutting acrylic that for all practical purposes they cannot be employed. They are awkward and difficult to use, and present hazards for the user.

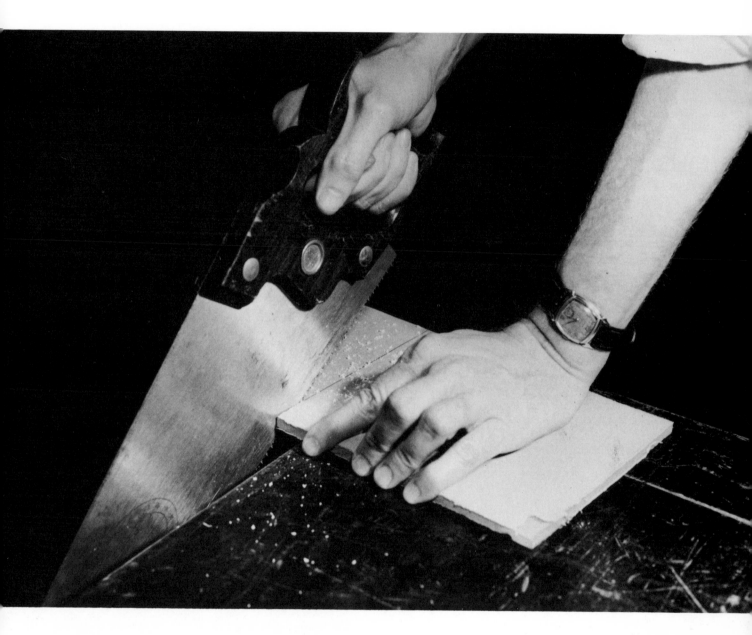

A straight cut with an ordinary hand saw is perfectly possible, though finer-toothed hand saws or machine tools will make a more precise cut.

TURNING, ROUTING, DRILLING, & ROTARY CARVING

Acrylic can be turned on power lathes. Lathe sizes vary from miniatures used by jewelers to large floor models used in production machining operations. A ten-inch bench wood lathe is satisfactory for ordinary use. Acrylic is turned in the same general manner as wood or brass, resulting in a semi-matte finish. Cutting tools should have a zero or negative rake angle to prevent chipping or gouging the material.

Wood-shavers or routers can be used to finish cut surfaces and to cut holes of various shapes. Portable hand routers are useful for trimming edges of sheets of thermoformed pieces and for surface routing of designs on the sheet or formed part; in fact, they are particularly useful when the part is too large or awkward to bring to the stationary router. Shaver and router cutters must be sharp and have a back clearance angle of approximately ten to thirty degrees positive rake for best operational results. The plastic should be fed slowly and continuously.

Standard drill presses and portable hand drills may be used for drilling acrylic. Twist-drill bits used for soft metals are satisfactory. But a better surface can be obtained if the drill bits are reground to zero rake so they have a scraping instead of a cutting action. An oil-and-water mixture, or compressed air, can be used as a coolant if needed.

To carve acrylic, sections are scraped away rather than cut as is the case with wood. Hand motor tools that drive small rotary cutters and burrs are useful.

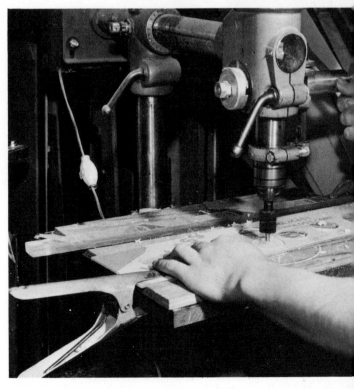

The twist drill and the adjustable hole cutter work well in acrylic.

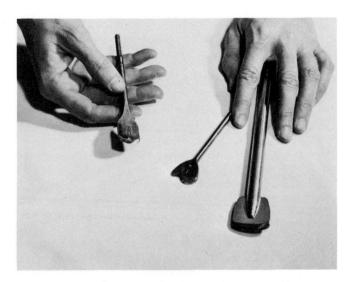

It is interesting to experiment with power tools. I made these special routers from ordinary high-speed bits. They make neat indentations on sheet acrylic. Left rough, these indentations disperse light and cast shadows. Polished, they act as unrefined lenses.

THERMOFORMING PROCESSES

One of the most interesting and useful characteristics of thermoplastics, especially for the artist and craftsman, is that thermoplastics become soft and pliable when sufficiently heated. Acrylic will soften when heated to temperatures ranging from approximately 250° to 340°F. At this stage, it becomes as soft and flexible as a sheet of gum rubber. It can then be pressed into a mold, vacuum formed or blowformed, or shaped by hand. Once the newly formed piece is cool, it stiffens, becomes rigid, and retains its new form.

Solid acrylic plastic can be stretched and formed into virtually any desired shape. However, because of the nature of the heat-forming process, it can be used only in sheet form for thermoforming. The bulk of thermoforming is done with extruded sheet, which stretches more easily and is less expensive than sheets made by casting, calendering, and laminating. However, cast acrylic sheet has some advantages; it has little tendency to shrink during cooling and it will produce articles of high optical clarity, with fewer internal stresses than extruded, calendered, and laminated acrylic. Therefore it is obviously more suitable for objects requiring these qualities.

Acrylic has an "elastic memory." If the newly created thermoformed shape is reheated to its forming temperature, it will return to its original shape, in this instance, the sheet. Because of this property of acrylic, the artist can reheat and reform the piece of plastic almost endlessly. In other words, the material offers the possibility of repeated reuse.

The thermoforming process is readily adaptable to studio and experimental work. Molds and mold design modifications are easy enough to make using simple tools and equipment, and the process is also suited to high-volume mass production. Such conditions offer many possibilities for the artist: he can create unique pieces, or he can just as easily go into mass production, as it were, and produce multiple objects, or he can create sculpture and other work made up of repeated forms.

Forming acrylic involves shaping it. Many forming processes are done entirely by hand, or with the aid of simple tools and equipment such as vises and clamps. Other thermoforming methods involve molds and more sophisticated forming equipment, such as permanently installed heating units and vacuum engines.

There are many variations in method and equipment, but the three basic methods of thermoforming are based on the means used to stretch the heated sheet onto a mold. They are mechanical forming (including simple bending), vacuum forming, and blowforming. Most industrial or art work of any complexity is made by some combination and adaptation of these methods and variations of them. Each type is discussed below with a general description of the process and its characteristics. The selection of a forming method will depend on the size, shape, thickness, and optical quality required for the formed part, as well as the equipment available.

BENDING & MECHANICAL FORMING

Bending is the simplest forming method and usually involves heat, although it is possible to bend the material cold if the bends are simple. This is not actually a thermoforming process, of course. For cold forming, unheated sheets of acrylic are bent by springing the plastic to simple and slight cylindrical shapes and securing them in a frame or jig until the plastic has been distorted. The radius of the curvature should be at least 180 times the thickness of the sheet. Sharper bending of unheated acrylic may result in stress crazing.

Heat bending is the only thermoforming method in which the entire sheet is *not* heated uniformly. The heat-bending process consists of heating the acrylic sheet locally to soften the section to be bent to a forming temperature. The sheet is then bent to the desired angle, and held by hand or in a jig until cool and rigid. Simple jig and clamp arrangements permit forming of a variety of shapes that require a bending operation only. Bending is usually used for small pieces where the length of the bend is relatively short. Short bends will retain their straightness and accuracy, but long bends will tend to bow over a period of time; this may be a handicap for the artist, since it will eventually distort his work.

The simplest method of heating acrylic for bending along a straight line is to use a strip heater, which locally heats the plastic to a forming temperature. (Strip heaters are discussed below in the section on thermoforming equipment.)

Drape forming

Drape forming is a mechanical forming process in which the acrylic sheet is uniformly heated until it becomes soft and rubbery, at which time it is draped over a mold and held in position until it cools and becomes rigid. The acrylic sheet is apt to "crawl"—the edges of the sheet will shrink and move away from the contour edges of the mold toward the center of the piece being formed. To help force the hot acrylic sheet to take the shape of the mold and to prevent crawling, the edges of the sheet should be held securely against the mold flange until the plastic has formed. A ring shaped to the contour of the mold is sometimes used for this purpose. It is brought down over the hot acrylic sheet, secured in position along the edges of the mold, and left until the formed part becomes rigid. The operator may use C-clamps or other spot-clamping devices to secure the edges; however, they do not provide as uniform an edge as do ring clamps and may result in malformations. After cooling, the formed part is removed from the mold, trimmed, and finished.

Sometimes it may be necessary for the operator to rub the hot sheet on the mold to bring the acrylic to the mold contour.

Cotton gloves should be worn to protect the operator's hands and to prevent fingerprinting the plastic. The operator may also rub the sheet with a pad of soft lint-free cloth.

VACUUM FORMING

Vacuum forming is a process in which a sheet of acrylic is shaped to the contours of a mold by the combination of heat and vacuum.

The mold may be either convex or concave and can be made of plaster of Paris, wood, or any other reasonably durable material. The shaped surface of the mold is vented by exhaust ports, which should be evenly distributed across the face of the mold for a uniform draw and to effect rapid air evacuation. All air spaces, other than exhaust ports, must be sealed so that when a vacuum is created the air in the cavity between the mold and the acrylic sheet will be drawn through the exhaust ports. Then outside atmospheric pressure forces the preheated sheet against the contours of the mold. A hold frame or clamping ring should be used to prevent the edges of the plastic from moving away from the base shape and to seal the hot flexible sheet against the flange of the mold.

The even, optimum draw-down, the exact registration, the sharper definition, and the optical clarity obtained by this process make the technique desirable for forming shapes to be used when accuracy is desirable or necessary.

Another method is to place the vacuum table beneath the heat source, cover the mold with a piece of polyethylene, and seal the edges of the polyethylene to the table with tape. After heat is applied and the acrylic sheet is soft, the vacuum motor should be started to create a vacuum to pull the polyethylene cover down over the hot, soft acrylic sheet, forcing it to the contours of the mold. The heat is then removed, but the vacuum is maintained until the acrylic piece is cool.

There are vacuum-forming machines of varying sizes on the market, but machines capable of doing large-scale work are expensive. It is possible to build a forming machine using an industrial tank-type vacuum cleaner for vacuum pressure, and the forming process itself is a relatively simple one and can be done in the studio. However, because of costs, space requirements, and probable infrequent use of this method, the artist is more likely to design the mold and have a plastics shop fabricate the piece.

BLOWFORMING

Blowforming is also based on an air-pressure differential and is essentially the reverse of the process used in vacuum forming. The heated acrylic sheet is positioned directly over a mold and clamped to its edges; then compressed air pressure, applied from above the hot sheet, forces the plastic to conform to the mold surface. Air pressure is kept constant until the acrylic sheet takes the shape of the mold and has cooled and hardened. The formed piece is then removed, trimmed, and finished.

The same equipment is necessary for blowforming as for vacuum forming, and molds are of equal complexity; thus, the expenses are comparable. Molds used in both processes must be sturdily constructed, because of the force of the air pressure applied to them.

Free blowforming

Blowforming can also be accomplished by applying air pressure from below the hot sheet. The shape created is determined by the shape of the hole in the clamping device, and its size is determined by the length of time air pressure is applied; no mold is required. Air pressure must be kept constant until the form cools and is hard.

This process is especially well suited for the creation of freeform shapes, and, in the hands of a skilled technician, can be so exact as to permit him to repeat the same shape.

The same equipment is needed for free blowforming as for mold blowforming, but instead of a mold a simple flat sheet with a hole of any shape cut through it is used. The expense of the blower is the same, but since there is no mold, thermoforming is less complicated and requires fewer materials and less time for the construction of equipment. Thus, free blowforming is not as expensive as blowforming.

THERMOFORMING TEMPERATURES

Optimum temperature at which acrylic should be formed varies according to the thickness of the sheet, the forming method used, and the shape desired. The most appropriate temperatures for forming cast acrylic range between 320° and 340°F.

Care should be taken to avoid heating the sheet to too high a temperature or holding it at maximum forming temperature for too long a time, because excessive heating tends to yellow acrylic, and prolonged heating will break down the material structurally. Also, if the temperature is too high, blisters or other surface distortions may appear.

Thin sheets of acrylic must be heated to a higher temperature for forming than thick ones because they lose their heat more rapidly. "Cold forming," or forming at too low a temperature, will cause crazing and warping. For each 1/100 inch of thickness of acrylic sheet, one minute heating time should be allowed, and if forming cannot be completed before the temperature drops below 275°F., the mold should be pre-heated. For this reason, forming should take place in a warm enclosed area to increase working time.

THERMOFORMING EQUIPMENT

Two items of equipment are required in almost all thermoforming operations: a source of heat and a mold. Auxiliary components and equipment include various types of clamping frames to secure the sheet during heating, forming, and cooling; mechanical and automatic devices for moving and controlling heaters, molds, and sheeting; plus a platen, or base, to support the mold.

Strip heaters

A strip heater is a device to heat thermoplastics in a line only. In using such a heater, the acrylic sheet is placed over the heating element and allowed to remain until that section of the sheet becomes soft. Thick acrylic may need to be heated on both sides to bring it to the correct temperature for bending. The plastic is then bent to the required shape and held by hand or mechanical means until cool, at which time it is ready to trim and finish. To avoid marring the surface of the acrylic, heating equipment should not make direct contact with the sheet.

Only in strip heating is it sufficient to spot-heat acrylic in isolated areas. For all other thermoforming processes the entire sheet should be uniformly heated to avoid the possibility of crazing and warping.

Strip heaters are commercially available, or can be constructed from resistance-type heating elements. Pressure steam lines or open-flame torches may also be used to soften the material for bending. When using a pressure steam line as a heating unit, the operator simply places the sheet over the pre-cushioned and insulated line and leaves it there until it is soft. It is obvious that with a torch, exact temperature control is not possible; therefore, the artist must be careful to avoid blistering or otherwise marring the acrylic surface, unless such distortions are desired. When using an open flame, the operator should be alert to fire hazards.

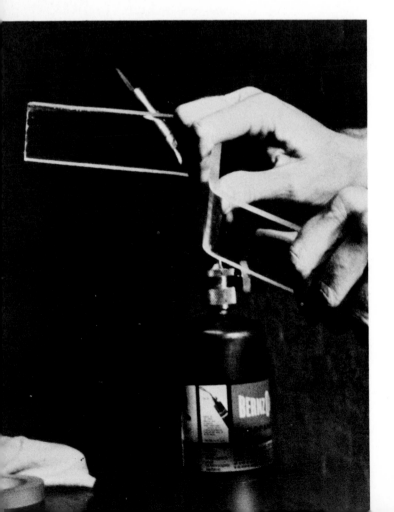

A piece of acrylic being formed by hand after being heated at the bend with a propane torch. One must be careful not to overheat the acrylic or it will bubble, and the piece must be held or clamped in position for some minutes until it cools or it will straighten out.

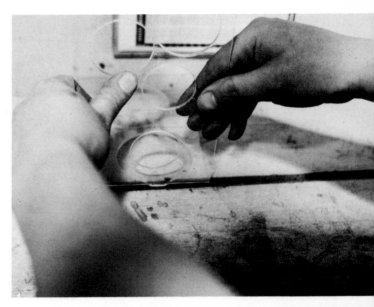

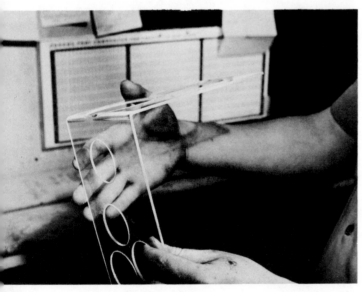

A simple strip-heating outfit may consist of an electrified rod set between, and slightly below the surface of, two planks. After a few minutes—the time depends on the thickness of the sheet and the temperature of the heater—a sheet placed over the rod will be soft enough to bend easily.

Ovens

An ordinary kitchen oven is often useful in heating small pieces of acrylic for the forming operation. Such ovens are usually thermostatically controlled and can easily be kept in the proper temperature range for forming. To avoid scarring the surface, the operator should place the piece to be formed on a cloth-covered tray.

If anything contacts the hot acrylic it will cause "mark-off"—an impression on the surface. In order to avoid mark-off, and other distortions, special ovens have been designed for heating thermoplastics that make provision for suspending the sheet vertically, rather than supporting it horizontally as in a kitchen oven. Before the sheet is inserted into the oven, it is attached to a rod, which, in turn, slides into a runner on the oven ceiling. Such an arrangement allows the sheet to swing free and clear, and air can circulate readily around it. Or, of course, the sheet may be heated as in an ordinary kitchen oven by laying it flat on soft flannel.

An oven equipped with a fan, commonly called a forced-air-circulation oven, is preferred in order to ensure uniform heating of the acrylic sheet. Such an oven should be regulated thermostatically.

Ovens are more commonly powered by electricity or gas than by any other source, but steam and infrared are adequate heating methods as well. In fact, almost any means of heat may be used to operate the oven, but all ovens should be equipped with automatic temperature regulators.

Suspended heaters

A heating unit mounted directly above the acrylic sheet (which is, in turn, suspended above the mold and platen) is a more satisfactory heating device than an oven, where the sheet must be removed and brought to a mold. The primary advantage of such a heating and work arrangement is that there is no loss of heat in moving the sheet, so the method allows for immediate forming when the acrylic has reached its minimum forming temperature, eliminating the risks of yellowing or other distortions caused by prolonged heating at excessive temperatures. Infrared or electrical radiant heating panels are commonly used in such heating devices.

An adjustable metal or wood clamping frame is needed to hold the sheet during heating, and in order to compensate for sheet shrinkage, it should be left on the sheet and clamped in place along the edge of the mold during the forming operation.

A means of removing the heating unit from above the acrylic when it has reached the proper temperature for forming is necessary so that the operator can proceed immediately with the actual thermoforming process. If the heater is mounted on a swing or a sliding bar above the work area, the operator may simply swing or slide the heater out of his way. The heating unit also may be mounted on a pulley and lifted to the studio ceiling, provided the ceiling is high enough to allow the heater to clear the work area sufficiently.

The beginning of a series of experiments with odd scraps of ¼" acrylic heated in an ordinary oven. A towel is wrapped around a sheet of asbestos to prevent mark-off; if it is left in the oven too long it will scorch and burn.

The heated piece is taken out of the oven with folded handkerchiefs—gloves would be handier—and twisted. It must be held until it cools or it will quickly flatten.

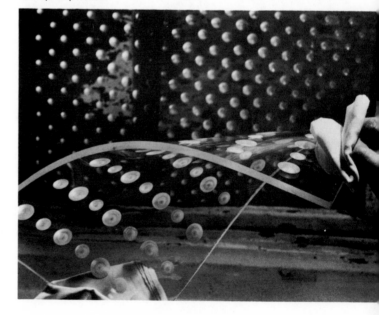

Another experiment with a sheet of ⅛" acrylic. The sheet was put over a bottle and allowed to drape naturally when it reached forming temperature. The resulting shape was a simple arc, so the sheet was further deformed by pressing it around the bottle to form a scoop. This shape did not seem interesting enough to keep either, so the sheet was put back in the oven and allowed to flatten. Note that the near edge has bubbled because the oven was too hot.

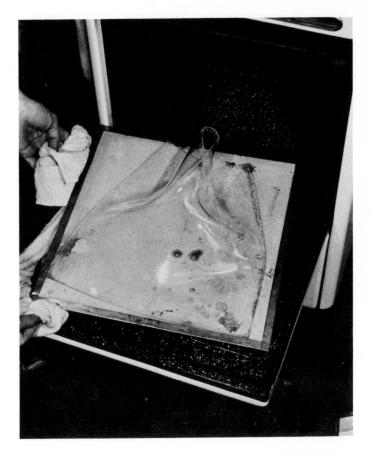

To see what further effects overheating would cause to the sheet, it was left in awhile at the same temperature. It made a noise like popcorn, and soon both surfaces were evenly pitted with white. Here the sheet is being rolled into a cylinder.

A vise is used to squeeze the end of the tube so that it will fit into another shape formed earlier. In this flattened section the white pits seemed to be suspended at several distinct levels in a solid bar—an effect that might be worth achieving deliberately.

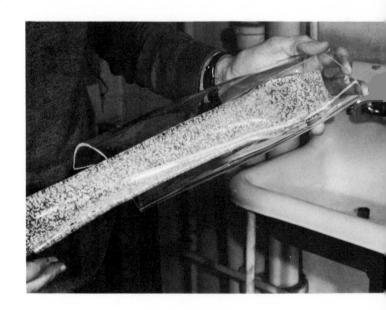

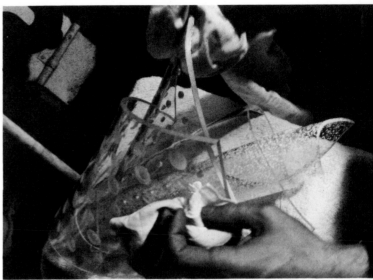

This scrap piece had been drilled through and the edges had been painted bright yellow with acrylic paint so that the color glowed from the unpainted but roughened holes. It was heated carefully, because any overheating would discolor the paint.

Here the last piece, still hot and flexible, is slipped inside the piece formed first and allowed to cool in place. Is the result a sculpture? The pieces can always be separated and reheated to their original forms, and the experimenter can try again. The smell of cooking acrylic is somewhat like fresh bread.

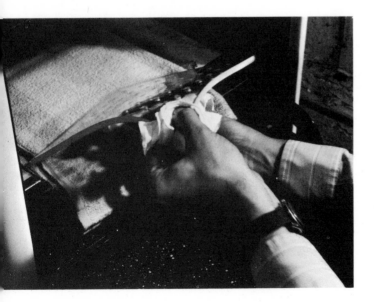

MOLDS

The act of thermoforming itself is relatively simple and quickly done. The creative, skilled, and often time-consuming work in making a thermoformed piece is in designing and constructing the molds, which cause the hot acrylic sheet to take the shapes the artist desires. The quality of the finished piece is largely determined by the care with which molds are made and used.

The basic shape made by thermoforming is an open, hollow, thin-walled object. Smooth convex shapes of large radius and straight lines, designed with curved edges, corners, and fillets, are more suitable to the nature of the material, and are consequently the easiest shapes to thermoform.

Because the hot acrylic sheet is stretched to the contours of the mold, the plastic will be thinner in certain sections after thermoforming than before. The thinnest part of the formed object will be the area furthest from the base section of the mold; that is, the bottom of the concave part, or the tip of the convex section. The deeper such indentions, or the higher the protrusions, the greater will be the thinning. Not only are depressions and protrusions of small diameter difficult to produce, but the finished thermoformed piece may be next to impossible to remove from convex molds because sheet shrinkage may lock it to the mold. On the other hand, even the minimal amount of sheet shrinkage which occurs in cast acrylic causes the sheet to pull away from concave cavities as it cools, making it easy to remove such pieces from the mold.

Thermoformed designs which contain large flat areas or thin wall sections have a greater impact strength than similarly designed injection-cast acrylic work. Even so, the completed piece may lack flexural strength, which is the pressure in pounds necessary to break a given sample of a material when applied to the center of the sample while it is supported at both ends. For this reason, it is helpful to form corrugations, or reinforcing ribs, when the design will allow, to increase the rigidity of flat areas. Not only will reinforcing strengthen the piece, but it will also enable the artist to use thinner acrylic, thus making the work lighter in weight and less expensive to produce.

Any material that will not decompose at the forming temperatures of acrylic may be used to make molds. However, because of its ready availability, comparative inexpensiveness, and ease of use, the artist will find plaster of Paris a good all-round material for most mold-construction purposes. Other materials that may prove satisfactory are wood, metal, and various plastics. A pliable material that allows for design changes and alterations during mold construction and slow, uniform cooling of the formed piece is preferred.

Even though cast acrylic tends to shrink very little, all molds should be built oversize to allow for shrinkage when the piece cools from the forming temperature to room temperature.

A shrinkage allowance of approximately 3/32 inch per foot is adequate. Also it is desirable to cut the acrylic sheet larger than the mold to assure that it will still extend beyond the trim line after forming is completed and cooling has occurred.

No matter how carefully the surface of the mold has been smoothed it is still likely to leave some mark-off on the surface of the plastic that it contacts. For this reason, if the surface of the thermoformed piece is to be smooth, the mold should be covered with a soft material containing as little texture as possible. Mold surfaces covered with cotton flannel or felt decrease mark-off adequately for most purposes and keep the surface of the plastic smooth, clean, and unmarred. If an embossed pattern or other texture is desired on the piece, it should be incorporated into the surface of the mold.

The mold designer should consider the fact that in stretching, the plastic sheet tends to bridge across detail on the mold surface, and that the thickness of the sheet determines the amount of detail produced. With thin sheets, very fine detail is possible; thicker sheets pick up less detail. Maximum sheet thickness to emboss surface patterns, during thermoforming is usually about a quarter inch.

In vacuum and blowforming the mold is subjected to much greater force than in other thermoforming methods, so it should be constructed of a sturdy, durable material that will resist breakage. A good heat-conduction material will facilitate by helping to allow proper cooling of the formed part. Wood and plaster of Paris are both suitable because of their pliability and heat-conducting characteristics.

The mold is prepared in the ordinary manner, but in addition it must be vented so that the hot acrylic sheet can be pulled, drawn, or blown uniformly and rapidly into recesses. Vents, or exhaust holes, should be located in the deepest mold crevices where air might be trapped, and they should be small enough to prevent hole marks on the plastic. The need for holes in the mold proper may be eliminated if the mold is designed so that venting occurs around shims.

Male molds

A convex, or male, mold generally costs less to build, is easier to use, and is more suitable for forming deep draw parts than is a concave, or female, mold. Also, because of its positive shape, working changes in mold design are usually easier to make in male than in female molds. Since the convex side of the sheet being formed does not contact the mold, male molds should be used when the clearest optical surface, embossing or other type of decoration, is desired on the convex side of the formed piece.

Female molds

A female, or concave, mold is used when the best optical surface, or a pre-decorated surface, must be on the concave side of the formed piece, because that side of the plastic sheet does not contact the mold. Ordinarily, a female mold should not be used for parts requiring a draw of greater than one-half the width of the part.

Matched molds

A matched mold consists of a male and a female mold shaped to control both sides of the sheet being formed. It is the only forming process that allows the production of detail on each side of the sculpted piece. The mold is calibrated to produce the required thickness of the piece to be formed and its surfaces are patterned, textured, or smoothed, as the case may be, to create the surface quality wanted by the artist.

Mold designs usually should not deviate too far from the fluid, flexible quality of acrylic. Work which calls for sharp corners, right-angle edges, or other angular sections and points should not be produced by thermoforming, because acrylic tends to thin excessively and to tear in these areas of stress concentration.

Mold bases

In most thermoforming operations, the platen, or support for the mold, is constructed of metal, primarily because of its strength. Other durable materials may be used; however, they aren't as substantial or as fireproof. If vacuum forming or blowforming is to be done in the studio or shop, the platen should contain an outlet for air pressure or vacuum.

BONDING

A considerable amount of solid acrylic sculpture and other design work is a consequence of the structural manipulation of preformed or commonly available parts. Much of this finished structure is simply a result of aesthetic decisions regarding shapes and sizes to be combined. It is possible to achieve a great variety of surprisingly complex effects derived solely from such manipulation. However, it is important to note here, before any commentary on the nature of acrylic bonding, two important points. First, typical household cements or other adhesives, such as are commonly used in woodworking, will not produce a permanent bond when cementing acrylic to acrylic. Second, the flow properties of non-acrylic materials to be joined to acrylic must be very close to that of acrylic to effect cohesive bonding.

A box being bonded together in the shop. Such a bond must be clamped delicately; too much pressure will squeeze the solvent out of the joint.

Cohesive cementing

A cohesive solvent cement is needed when joining acrylic to acrylic. In cohesive cementing the molecules of the surfaces being bonded are actually caused to intermingle by the solvent action of the cement. Unlike adhesive cements, no foreign substances lies between the united surfaces, and as the solvent penetrates and evaporates, the two softened areas actually flow together and fuse. It is like welded metal.

Cohesive agents are solvent cements and polymerizable monomers, such as ethylene dichloride, methylene dichloride,

methyl methacrylate monomer, or epoxy-type cements. Chloroform is another agent that may be used, as well as glacial acid and acetone. However, it should be pointed out that the strong solvent action of these three can easily cause crazing and "blushing"—a clouding or whitening of the acrylic surface due to a chemical reaction of the acrylic to the solvent or its fumes.

The parts to be cemented should have unpolished, slightly abraded surfaces and must be aligned accurately. They should not be buffed, as buffing tends to round off edges, causing an uneven fit with less surface-to-surface contact.

After the edges have been brought into contact and cemented, the assembly is held firmly in a jig or other holding arrangement until the solvent has penetrated the surfaces being joined and all traces of it have evaporated and the joint has hardened. Usually, this takes place in a matter of minutes, but it can take several hours, depending on the particular cement employed and the nature and type of joint. Care should be taken to apply only enough pressure to remove air bubbles from the joint. Too much pressure will squeeze out part of the cement, leaving dry spots. Small pieces can be hand-held or taped or tied together to supply the necessary pressure; larger pieces, of course, require a more elaborate method of holding, such as some sort of jig arrangement.

The temperature of the parts being cemented and the temperature and humidity conditions of the work area are important considerations. A joint made under high humidity conditions will be cloudy because of moisture condensation. When the rate of evaporation is too rapid, the solvent will disappear before it has had time to soften the plastic. This results in an imperfect bond. In addition, the fumes resulting from rapid evaporation may attack the surface of the plastic, causing blushing or in extreme cases crazing—which may not become apparent until hours, days, or even weeks after cementing.

Cements vary as to speed of action, strength of bond, and ease of application. With some experimentation it is possible to adjust the speed with which any given cement performs. For example, acrylic chips can be added to the thin, watery solvents to make a desirably slower-acting cement. The strength of the joint will reflect the type of cement and cementing technique used and whether or not the finished piece is annealed. Its appearance and permanence will depend on the avoidance of internal stresses, the proper preparation of the surfaces to be bonded, the proper cement, and correct cementing technique.

If a cement job is carefully executed with appropriate media and technique, the result is a joint that is virtually invisible. Further, if done well, it ordinarily requires no post-treatment, or annealing. Finally, the well-executed cementing of parts results in a single unit possessing approximately 75 percent of the tensile strength of a solid sheet of acrylic.

My homemade routers make it very easy to attach an acrylic sphere to the surface of a sheet. Even though the routed indentation is not polished, the bond between indentation and sphere is clear.

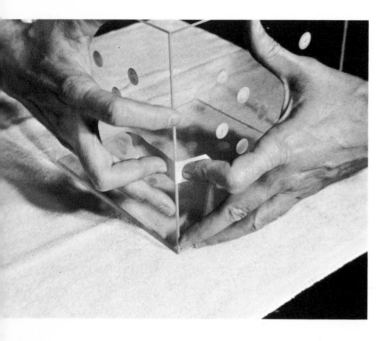

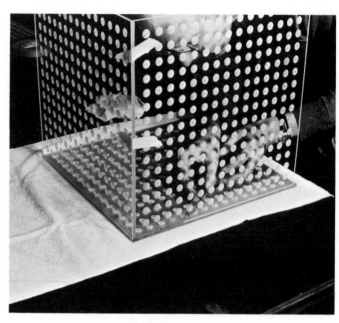

Pieces that do not need much strength can be joined simply by taping them and applying solvent with a brush. Capillary action draws the solvent into the joint. Note that the joints here are beveled, which creates a lighter and more precise effect than butted joints.

A larger box with butted joints being bonded with solvent and a hypodermic syringe. The bond sets up almost immediately.

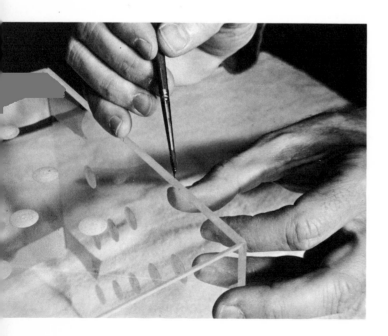

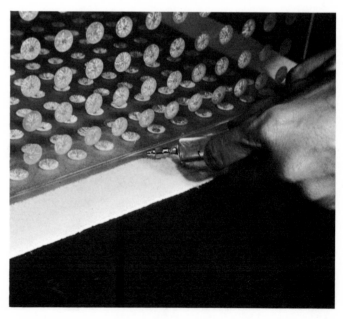

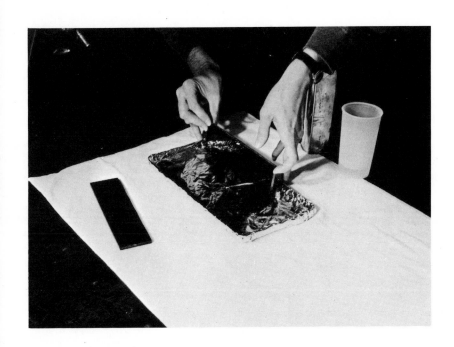

A very strong joint can be obtained by soaking an edge in a tray of solvent. Here the tray is simply a plastic lid covered with aluminum foil. The edge will swell and become rubbery, and it can then be pressed to a dry acrylic surface and clamped until the bond sets.

Soak cementing

As the term suggests, soak cementing is a process in which the edge of a piece to be joined is allowed to soak in a solvent long enough to soften and swell into a cushion caused by a chemical reaction of the acrylic to the solvent. The time required to produce the cushion, or softened layer, will vary according to three factors involved in the bonding: the cement used, the type of joint to be made, and the thickness of the sheet soaked. This can be as brief as half a minute or as long as a quarter of an hour. When an adequate cushion has been formed, the two edges to be bonded, one wet with solvent, the other dry, are pressed together immediately, before the solvent has had time to evaporate. The cushion holds the solvent needed to swell the opposite dry surface, causing molecular action that fuses the two pieces into a solid. Care must be taken not to leave the acrylic in the solvent for too long, or it will form a cushion that is so deep that the softened acrylic will extrude, causing scars or an ill-fitting joint.

Soak cementing produces strong permanent joints that can withstand heavy loads and extremes of temperature and climatic conditions. It is also a useful method to help close joints that are not perfectly fitted. However, bonding should not be relied upon to cover up poor machining.

Capillary cementing

In capillary cementing the solvent is introduced to the butted edges of the joint with any common small applicator, such as a paint brush or syringe. After capillary action has spread the cement to all parts of the joint, light pressure should be used to hold the assembly together until molecular action has fused the pieces.

Capillary cementing provides a quick and easy way of assembling parts which proves satisfactory for most ordinary purposes. However, the strength of the joint is variable; therefore, it is not a method recommended for the cementing of pieces which may be subjected to heavy loads or severe or continuous weathering.

Cementing other materials to acrylic

In most cases, even though there is a substantial difference in thermal expansion between acrylic and nonplastic materials, strong bonds between them may be obtained with cohesive solvents provided the flow properties of the two materials are similar.

Other types of adhesives and cements may also be used but the operator must keep in mind that when exposed to fluctuating temperatures, the two materials expand and contract by different amounts, placing heavy stresses on the bond. Cements which harden during aging are too rigid to maintain adhesion over a large temperature range; only ones which remain permanently elastic will continuously withstand the stresses set up by differential expansion and contraction of the joint.

Because they compensate for the differences in thermal expansion, remain elastic, and do not dry hard on aging, epoxy cements are especially useful for joining dissimilar materials to acrylic.

Masking

In order to protect the areas adjacent to the joint being bonded from the etching action of the cement, they should be covered with a special cellophane fiber tape or other coating impervious to the action of the solvent. The tape should be applied very carefully so that it is not possible for the cement to seep under its edges. Ordinary tape should not be used because it may inhibit the polymerization of the cement and in some cases cause discoloration of the cemented joint.

In cementing complicated sections where it is impossible to confine the spread of the solvent by tape, the area can be masked by a coating of a gelatin solution made from hide glue, glycerine, and water. More simply, rubber cement may be used for masking with most solvents.

Safety precautions

Solvent cements and fumes released from solid acrylic during machining are toxic, and the cements are inflammable. Inhaling the concentrated vapors of these volatile liquids and fumes for extended periods of time may cause illness; so the artist should provide a well-ventilated work area for cutting and for cementing operations. The work area should be away from any source of heat in order to avoid fire. Also, the artist should be cautioned not to put his hands in the solvents more often than is absolutely necessary, and he should wash thoroughly after any exposure to them.

FINISHING

Acrylic can be finished, as well as machined, by techniques similar to those used for woods and metals. The major difference is that acrylic will soften if frictional heat is generated during finishing. Continued sanding or polishing will cause the surface to melt. However, the use of a coolant will reduce melting. Finishing operations include filing, scraping, sanding, ashing, and buffing; each is described below.

Filing

Acrylic tends to clog standard mill files. A special single-cut file with a longer angle than the ordinary file (45° as compared to 60°) and a shear-tooth is recommended. Such a file has a wider gullet to provide greater chip clearance, eliminating clogging and melting.

Scraping

Cut edges can be scraped with an ordinary hand scraper. The acrylic should be held firmly and the blade inclined in the direction the scraper is to be moved. Scraping is all the finishing that is necessary when preparing pieces to be cemented, and in most other cases scraping provides an adequate finish, eliminating sanding and additional finishing procedures.

The hand scraper leaves a smooth matte finish on edges.

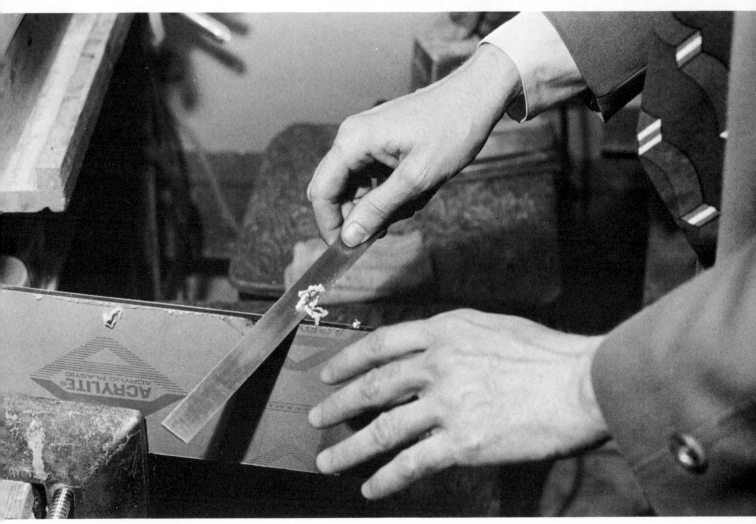

Sanding

The surface of acrylic should not be sanded unless the imperfections are too deep to be filled with tallow and made invisible by buffing—or unless, of course, the optical distortion resulting from sanding is desired.

The technique for sanding acrylic is essentially the same as that used for finishing wood. Because acrylic scratches easily, sanding is used primarily for preliminary finishing operations, or to shape or true a piece by removing desired amounts of the material before polishing.

A fine sandpaper should be used to remove imperfections: usually 320-A wet-or-dry sandpaper is as coarse as required and may be followed by 400-A or finer paper for smoother finishes. The sandpaper should be soaked in water for a few minutes before using, and kept wet while sanding. Water serves as a coolant reducing frictional heat, which could melt acrylic.

For the easiest hand sanding, the paper should be wrapped around a wood or hard-rubber block, and sanding should be done in a wide area to avoid creating recessed areas or pockets.

The same general procedures apply to machine sanding. Disk and belt sanders and grinding wheels are usually used on the edges rather than on the surface of the material. They can be used to true straight edges, and, in some instances, to shape curves. An oscillating sander is good for sanding pierced designs, while portable hand sanders work well for sanding small areas or large pieces of acrylic which are too awkward to manipulate around a fixed machine. To avoid overheating the material, 50- to 100-grit open-coat abrasives are used for machine sanding. Such a grit leaves a uniformly .scratched surface which may be satisfactory for some uses. Final sanding should leave the work satin-smooth and ready for other finishing operations required.

All in all, sanding is an awkward, time-consuming operation that I have found to be of limited value. The surface of acrylic is highly polished when it comes from the manufacturer and generally will require no treatment in the studio. The artist need only be concerned about truing edges or preparing them to be cemented. For these purposes scraping is usually sufficient.

Ashing

Ashing is a coarse buffing operation useful for removing rough spots and scratches. In some cases it can be used in place of sanding. It produces a satin-smooth surface, and little final finishing is required to obtain a high polish. For ashing a slurry of pumice and water is used on a moderately firm abrasive wheel made of stitched cotton. Again I have found ashing to be of limited value. Usually scraping is all the preliminary finishing necessary prior to buffing.

Disk and belt sanders are excellent for truing straight edges and forming simple convex curves.

A small drum sander attached to the drill press is handy for sanding the edges of holes and concave curves.

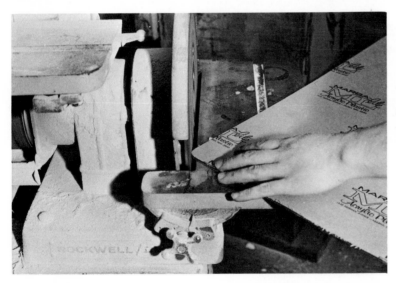

Rouge and a polishing wheel will leave an edge glassily transparent.

Buffing

Buffing is a polishing operation that is done after scraping, sanding, and ashing. The acrylic may be buffed with a dry cotton wheel that contains an abrasive. The coarseness of the abrasive used depends on the original roughness of the acrylic part as well as on the degree of luster desired. Buffing will not true the work being machined or eliminate scratches from the surface; instead it reaches into depressions and polishes them.

A separate wheel should be used for each abrasive grit, and acrylic parts should be washed and dried between buffings to remove abrasive deposits which would contaminate finer grit wheels. Care must be taken to avoid overheating the material with excessive speeds and pressures in machine buffing.

A large variety of commercial abrasives, usually composed of alumina in combination with wax, tallow, or grease binders, is available. Abrasives commonly used for buffing are tripoli and jeweler's rouge.

After successive buffings, when the scratches produced by the abrasive are sufficiently fine, the plastic should be buffed on a wheel to which only tallow has been applied. The tallow fills tiny scratches, making them less noticeable. The wheel should be of open unbleached cotton.

Final polishing is done by buffing with a clean wheel of unstitched flannel which will bring the acrylic to a high polish giving it a luster. In addition, wax applied to the surface with a soft cloth is sometimes used to complete the finishing operation.

CLEANING

Acrylic may be cleaned by simply washing it with a mild soap or detergent and rinsing with water. Plenty of water should be used to rinse the soap film from the surface, and the piece should be dried by wiping with the bare hands or a soft cloth or chamois.

To minimize the attraction of dust or other foreign material to the finished acrylic surface an antistatic cleaner may be applied to the surface. The fluid will also clean and polish the surface, leaving it clear, lustrous, and shining.

ANNEALING

Annealing consists of the prolonged heating of the machined or formed acrylic work at temperatures of at least 10°F. lower than those used for forming, followed by slow cooling. Internal stresses set up during machining or forming are reduced or eliminated by this treatment, which results in work of greater dimensional stability, greater resistance to crazing, and improved strength of cemented joints.

For the sake of expediency, annealing should be done in one operation, after the work is cemented, cleaned, and complete. However, this is not always possible, due to the size of the piece. In such cases, the parts to be assembled should be annealed separately, preferably no more than twenty-four hours before they are joined together.

Annealing is usually inconvenient as a studio practice. It is desirable, but properly processed, fabricated, and thermoformed acrylic work will contain low stress levels and show little improvement in joint strength or resistance to crazing or other distortions, and probably the added time and expense of annealing will be unnecessary.

A NOTE ON PLASTICS MERCHANTS

There are plastics specialty stores in most sizable communities across the country that stock a wide range of plastics—acrylic and other. Many lumber companies now have acrylic sheets, although their supply is usually limited, and it is likely that they will not carry more unusual colors and shapes such as cylinders, rods, and spheres. A source of supply for small boxes and other items might be local novelty and ten-cent stores.

In New York City, plastics merchants are mostly located below 14th Street. Amplast, Inc., 359 Canal Street, and Industrial Plastics Supply Co., 309 Canal Street, are excellent sources of supply, and both will fill mail orders. There are other plastic supply stores along Broadway and at Astor Place. Boroughs other than Manhattan do not have comparable outlets, but acrylic is available.

A NOTE ON BOOKS ABOUT ACRYLIC

There are three types of books about plastic that include discussions of acrylic. One, completely technical, is written for industry and in no way deals with the material as an expressive, aesthetic medium for art and design work. There is a vast amount of this literature, most of it published directly after World War II when we expected plastics would replace a good many other more familiar materials. Such books may sometimes be of value to the artist or designer who already has a considerable knowledge of acrylic and wants to solve specific technical problems.

Another type of book is directed to teachers and their pupils—"how-to-do-it" books consisting of patterns of shelves, letter holders, and other do-dads to be constructed of acrylic. The educational value of these books is slight—perhaps they are even downright harmful—and for that reason they could not be recommended even if they contained topical or useful information. These too for the most part were issued immediately following World War II.

Recently there have been a few good thorough books about plastics in general that thoughtfully consider acrylic as a material for aesthetic use. Among the more helpful are: Thelma Newman, *Plastics as an Art Form* (Philadelphia: Chilton, 1964), an almost encyclopedic work in which one chapter and part of another is devoted to acrylic; and Nicholas Roukes, *Sculpture in Plastics* (New York: Watson-Guptill, 1968), which, like Newman's book, is general, but deals in three chapters with the material. Robert S. Swanson, *Plastics Technology* (Bloomington: McKnight, 1956), is a clearly written, well-illustrated guide to working with plastic, including acrylic. In addition, the Society of the Plastics Industry and the Society of Plastics Engineers publish good concise instructions for working the material, and so do Rohm and Haas and DuPont.

AFTERWORD

Acrylic intrigues Sylvia Stone because of the flatness of the sheet. It intrigues Aleksandra Kasuba because of the light it transmits and the shadows it can cast. These are indeed intriguing properties—and perhaps the most intriguing thing about them is that they are so elusive. They are not just phenomena, but ideas, nontangible elements that have, traditionally, been more in the domain of the painter than of the sculptor. Sculpture has consisted of materials that are real and can be touched, picked up and moved about, walked around; materials that, because of their density, stop the viewer at their surface.

Acrylic is real, but it is ambiguous and ambivalent too. It does not have the surface monumentality of traditional sculptural materials; it is aesthetically flexible rather than hard and set. In fact, it is possible to lose acrylic visually even while looking at it; one reacts to the "absence" of the material rather than to its presence. In short, acrylic is apt to make its strongest impression not for what it is, but for what it *is not*.

But there is more to it than that. Mies van der Rohe's "Less is more" is an important concept in modern aesthetics and the basis for much work. Nevertheless, the simplest means of construction and the sparest use of materials are not ends in themselves. They are only means to "more"—more richness and more involvement.

My first experiences with acrylic were very casual. Small colored and clear boxes of acrylic were just beginning to be seen in novelty stores. The material was so clean and clear, the colors so pure yet unusual—colors that simply were not available in any other material. I made a series of hand sculptures of these boxes and other small acrylic objects. A blue box and a yellow box might be contained by a larger green one, creating elusive new colors and shapes. The small boxes might be full of spheres of various sizes, or they might contain half-spheres that barely fit between two different-colored surfaces so that they move haltingly when the box was handled, while a single small ball raced past in another box or passage. Some boxes each had one small sphere that plinks when the work is picked up and moved. Others had two or several spheres of different sizes, making different sounds and movements.

Another early piece was a wandlike tube with three spheres that exactly fit inside. When the wand was moved the spheres would move too, at different speeds, always changing their relationship to one another. Somehow, kinetics always seemed a part of the material to me—whether there was actual movement, as in my early hand sculptures, or optical illusion of movement that depended on the viewer's movement, as in my later pieces.

One thought that occurred to me quite early was to use the optical properties of acrylic in painting by making a lenslike structure to look through. I routed concavities in a sheet of acrylic, polished them, and ended up with a whole panel of concave lenses of different sizes, from very small toward the edges of the sheet to much larger in the center, which produced the illusion that the sheet was thick in the center and gradually thinned toward the edges, like a giant convex lens. There are similar concavities, though unpolished ones, in much of my work now—but I have not gone further with polished lenses, because this early effort combining painting and acrylic sculpture seemed to me a complete failure. Nevertheless, the sheet of lenses, as well as being an interesting experiment, has been a success of a sort: I used it to replace a broken window pane. I painted the flat areas of the sheet red,

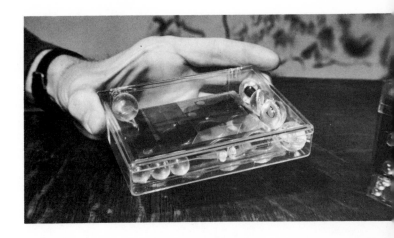

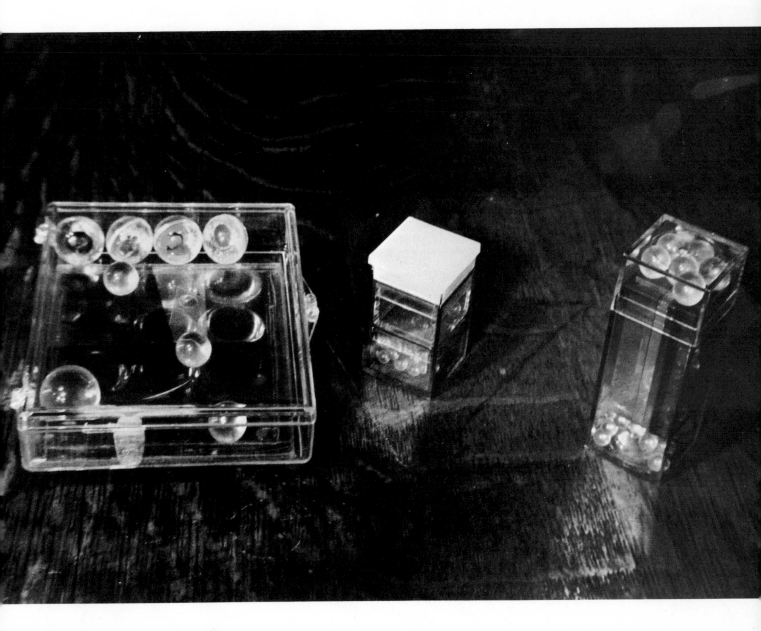

leaving the lenses clear; it is always sparkling and changing with the light, making its presence felt throughout the room.

Recently I cast some acrylic spheres inside a cube of polyethylene. Polyethylene is less transparent than acrylic, so the acrylic spheres inside seem hollow and more opaque, rather than solid and clear; they look strangely heavy and static. Here and there one of the spheres breaks the surface of the cube, and in these areas it looks as if the polyethylene resin had been cut away. The cube contains a few small colored objects, and when one looks directly into a protruding sphere the interior dimensions and coloration of the cube change dramatically, each small alteration in angle or distance of view producing a different contained world. It is something like focusing a microscope at high power down through a drop of pond water: each tiny adjustment with the focusing wheel makes one slice of microscopic life disappear and another appear. As frequently with acrylic sculpture, there is an intimate relationship between viewer and object, and no two viewers ever get exactly the same view.

Like many acrylic sculptors, I have most recently been cutting and assembling the material in the manner of the Constructivists. Flat sheets assembled into a sealed cube create, for me, a far richer world than one would imagine possible from such simple and austere means. The interior seems devoid of air, untouched, inaccessible to the outside world, and it has a charmlike, almost hypnotic fascination for me. Sometimes the cubical space contains geometrical patterns worked on the inner surfaces of the sheets, which combine in further moiré patterns. Sometimes it contains transparent shapes that seem to float or to cling to the sides of the cube as though held by static electricity. Several identical boxes become modules which can be rearranged either by me or by a viewer, creating various patterns which are open to new and varied interpretations.

In order to develop and elaborate upon the enclosed-world idea, I am working on a fountain that is an extension of the stacked-box sculpture, with the added elements of water and the dimension of time. The work will be made of edge-lighted cubes; a column of water will gush from the bottom cube and fill the top one, before it drips into a middle cube, partially filling it, and then drips into and fills the bottom section. The piece will keep its aloofness in the sense of being a world contained; the water will be enclosed and consequently inaccessible to the viewer. Another part, water, will be incorporated into the enclosed world of the sculpture, and time will be made visible by the movement of water. It must be noted, however, that this work is fixed and will not permit viewer rearrangement of the modules.

To reverse the enclosed-space concept, I am using modular forms in greater numbers to create larger work. The idea is directed toward pieces of sculpture that will define and dominate the space in which they exist. These will take the form of huge man-made cubes that exceed human size and cause discomfort by their aggressiveness in relation to man and surrounding space.

I want one work to inhabit a whole room, to threaten the room, to make the surrounding space seem to fight for its existence. I want the spectator to feel that the work grows outward in all directions, uniformly and slowly, and that it is alive with a pulse and existence of its own. I want the spectator to feel threatened, to feel that he is trespassing, but to be so strongly attracted that he cannot easily leave once he has entered the gravitational field of the work. Such a piece of sculpture will activate external as well as internal space. In substance, it will be environmental.

My continuing discovery has been that acrylic, while it may seem objective and barren in its natural beauty, is highly expressive. Its semi-visibility, surface reflections, and other kinetic attributes appeal to my love of surprise and casual movement. Its pure, pristine surfaces suggest to me limitless possibilities—the perfect yet imperfect, somehow joyous world that can be enclosed within a rigid framework, the infinite yet sharply defined universe that can become visible in three dimensions. For me, an acrylic object can be utterly abstract, yet most intensely felt.

INDEX